D0498227

Donkey

The Mystique of *Equus Asinus*

MICHAEL TOBIAS
& JANE GRAY MORRISON

A DANCING STAR FOUNDATION BOOK

COUNCIL
OAK BOOKS

SAN FRANCISCO & TUCSON

A Dancing Star Foundation Book

First edition, first printing, 2006
Printed in Canada

Cover and interior design by Carl Brune

ISBN 1-57178-202-8
ISBN 978-1-57178-202-1

LIBRARY OF CONGRESS CATALOGING-IN-PUBLICATION DATA
Tobias, Michael.
    Donkey: the mystique of equus asinus / by Michael Tobias
    and Jane Gray Morrison.
        p. cm.
    "A Dancing Star Foundation Book."
    ISBN-13: 978-1-57178-202-1 (hardcover)
    ISBN-10: 1-57178-202-8   3488 638) 4/07
    1. Donkeys. I. Morrison, Jane Gray II. Title.
    SF361.T63 2006
    636.1'82–dc22
    2006026341

e dedicate this book to all those nameless donkeys who have populated this planet throughout time, asking nothing of the Earth other than that they should be free to be themselves. Their modesty, nobility and affection provided the inspiration and impetus for this work.

Contents

Acknowledgments

We wish to thank the dedicated staff of Dancing Star Foundation, particularly Jerry, Elaine and Tristen, for their daily love and protection of the donkeys in their care. Our special thanks to Don, to Karine and Samantha for research assistance, and to Maral. To our editor, Laura Wood, our highest esteem. And special thanks as well to her staff and publisher. Thanks to Carl Brune for his aesthetic sensibility and good taste. We wish also to thank those museums and individuals who kindly provided additional photographic materials. We particularly wish to acknowledge the inspired efforts of individuals at donkey sanctuaries throughout the world who are striving to make life better for the saintly *Equus asinus.*

Finally, we thank all those researchers involved with equines whose work has inspired us. Any inaccuracies that may have resulted from our own research and reliance on published data are our own errors, not those of individuals whose work we have endeavored to cite properly.

First Impressions

HOLMES

*T*his book has emerged out of our responses to donkeys: donkeys as a species and donkeys as individuals. The book grazes, feeding on a landscape both real and historical, imagined, desired and underfoot, inspired by a creature that has, strangely, embedded itself into the very fabric of philosophy, religion, art, the environment, human history, as well as in our hearts. Donkeys did not bray for this attention, but their own subtle beauty and gentleness have attracted our kind, while their "utility" has brought them loads of woe.

Our muse is the donkey, who wanders in our minds with calm, near lackadaisical, inward-thinking strides. This book is humble as donkeys may be perceived to be (though mules might argue the point). We two humans, each having had our own initiation with and by donkeys, wish to convey something of these extraordinary beings with whom we have the periodic pleasure of sharing our lives. Simply to be with them is a joy. We do not believe we can ever truly understand our mysterious friends, but then, what can we be said to fully know of any other person, even those closest and most beloved? It will be enough to gain the donkeys' trust and glean whatever insights they will allow of their inner worlds.

Our introductions to donkeys began many years ago.

Michael: "I must have been seven years old, with my parents driving from Colorado to California one summer. Somehow we ended up on a dirt road in the desert. I remember mountains on either side. There was no air conditioner in the car. Not in those days. The windows were open for ventilation. The temperature outside was hot, very hot, probably 110 degrees, maybe more. I felt the air to be heavy, menacing, and I was worried about the proposed picnic. It made little sense in terms of a rest stop, despite there being a turn-out, a picnic table, a concrete shelter and a couple of trees.

"There were flies tormenting the food, before it could even be removed from the Tupperware onto the red and white tablecloth my mother had brought along. Flies were at the brownies, the sandwiches, but worst of all, in my eyes and on my lips. In addition, little midges, or mosquitoes, rallied round my socks, getting to the skin beneath with annoying zeal.

"'How long do we have to stay here?' I asked my parents, who seemed intent upon a successful, if brief, outing.

"It was then that I first glimpsed a mirage approaching across the desert floor toward us: five wild animals, horse-like, but smaller, inquisitive, weather-beaten ghosts.

"Their tentative approach was fascinating to me. They conveyed an almost extraterrestrial presence. I could not imagine how such creatures survived what, to my way of thinking, was an ordeal just after a few minutes in such infernal temperatures.

"Remembering back to that first vague encounter, I know that what startled me the most was the desire to be near them; to engage them; to know them; to marvel at their vigor. In my mind's eye, I recall the original 'equipoise,' a gracefulness amid brutal surroundings.

"Little did I know that many years later I would marry a woman whose own first encounter with donkeys was also at a picnic table.

"Later on, such impressions were reinforced during a filming odyssey across central Arizona. Our team was in one of the most remote regions of the state, and there, once again, crossing the desert to inquire, was a small herd of wild burros. This time, they came very close, grazing on desert stubble, but wanting to join the party. They came only so close, however, retaining their autonomy in a manner that was declarative: You do not want to come any closer, I thought I heard. Or perhaps it was one of my own team suggesting it might not be the brightest idea to try and pet them. I didn't.

"Once, in highland Ladakh (Indian Tibet), I saw a herd of wild Tibetan asses, or Kiangs as they are called (*Equus kiang*), from a dusty Himalayan distance. They noticed me but showed only mild regard. The distance separating us was comprised of horrendous, cliff-tormented terrain, eighteen thousand feet in altitude, and they were busy. I could not imagine any more meaningful enterprise than gazing dreamily at their covey of nomadic meandering. There I clung to a forty-five-degree sheer ice wall with my twelve-point crampons and Chouinard ice axe, pinioned tentatively upon the doubtful surface where my life hung over a four thousand foot drop-off. Rock-fall from above posed another peril, as I was not in the custom of wearing a protective helmet. None of those risks mattered, not with wild Tibetan asses in the distance. My god, how beautiful they were. How dream-like in their hazy march across unimaginably difficult desert. What was their life all about? There could have been no greater imaginable urgency for me than to make their acquaintance. They were small, majestic, brilliant, wild, frolicking. And before I knew it, they were gone, as ephemeral as the wildest birds in migration, like some glimpse of the legendary Yeti."

Jane: "I suppose my first introduction to donkeys occurred when I was very small and my grandparents came to California and moved to a ranch in the foothills of a somewhat nearby mountain range. I was comfortable with the hazards of wild nature, having grown up, until that point, wild and free in a mountain canyon. Later, I lived for a year from the age of seven at a boarding school in the desert, wandering wherever I wished, always carrying the obligatory snake-bite kit. I feared having to make an incision in my own skin to draw out the snake's venom far more than I feared the rattler's bite. Fortunately, although I encountered many snakes, scorpions and a tarantula or two, I was never bitten. In the canyon where I grew up, I was always scaling cliffs. Neither I nor my parents gave a thought to the resident mountain lions. The worst experience I had was with poison oak. I got it repeatedly . . . very unpleasant!

"Still, the physical enormity of the domestic and semi-domestic pets—for all who dwelt in Grandma and Grandpa's sky haven were safe from human harm—overwhelmed me. There were cows, horses, a donkey or two, and the benign and beloved favorite of Grandpa, a water buffalo called 'Baby.' I remember frequent conversations with Baby, but most of my time was spent in the forest, wishing and imagining myself to be Snow White, visiting and visited by a myriad of small forest creatures, as I searched for frogs,

toads, lizards of any kind and
spoke with wildly loquacious
birds in response to their songs.
There I was at home.

"By the time Grandma and
Grandpa moved to the city, I had
read a translation of the heartbreakingly beautiful *Platero and I*,
and I dreamed of having such a donkey friend. I spoke of nothing
but Platero, who seemed gentler and more conscious and manage-
able than the horses I knew, those horses that I would never master, whom I feared for their size, but from whom I had never been
thrown. I abandoned the notion of becoming an equestrian before
I was eight, though I continued to ride with my brothers for some
years. What I really wanted, in addition to a baby elephant, was a
donkey like Platero: a friend who would understand my unspoken

MY FRIEND PLATERO

thoughts and dreams, a friend to walk by my side through life, a friend in whom I could confide completely, someone I could trust. To silence me, Mother and Father gave me a very beautiful German stuffed life-sized newborn miniature donkey. He was quite large. He fulfilled most of my expectations, was my best friend and was protected by me from all our ungainly or fractious pets (king-sized dogs, raccoons, an ape and a monkey, and several large parrots) and from my brothers' mischief. Of course, I named him Platero. He remains his perfectly beautiful self to this day.

"My first close encounter with donkeys happened when I was grown up or nearly so. With Michael, I visited a friend, who served us tea at a picnic table under an equine-ravaged tree. Her special treat for us was a personalized chocolate cake, our names inscribed in candy. Before we could make much of a dent in the cake we were surrounded; surrounded not by any of the other large creatures who freely roamed this land, but by a group of in-quisitive, sniffing, long-eared relatives of Platero. They were not too big, not too small, but as Platero would be, had he ever grown up; they were just right! No introductions were necessary, as I knew and welcomed all relatives of my best friend. They joined us. More plates were set at the picnic table, more mugs scrounged for libations, and a group of surprisingly well-behaved, thoroughly en-titled donkeys, made themselves at home in what seemed to me the most delightful and truly normal tea party it has been my plea-sure to attend. When the donkeys had polished off the last of the cake, we searched for other treats. A carton of dog biscuits was produced, and after a group of large muzzles turned themselves up at it, they dug in.

"It was for me a dream come true: Platero's relatives come to call—in life! I fell in love again, remembered my real self and found a true extended family of giant-sized 'puppy dogs.' Each donkey embodied the wisdom and wit of H. H. Munro's 'beyond cat,' Tobermorey, but each had the good sense to converse with me in a secret language that would not betray our honest exchange in the presence of adults.

SILVER AND BLACKIE AT TEA

"That most delightful of all madly delightful tea parties was to change my life forever."

DONKEY TEA PARTY

Given what science has learned, what poets have felt, and what great works of art and spirituality have conveyed, it astounds us to contemplate the degree to which donkeys and mules have suffered in their long history with humankind. But as it always seems with humans, even during our darkest moments, there is at least one person who allows him- or herself to be touched and to act on behalf of another being. For example, donkeys and mules were shoved into battle, where they experienced the same horrors over the centuries as human soldiers and innocent human civilians. During the Battle of Gallipoli on the Turkish peninsula during World War I, heroic donkeys and mules were used by the British forces to evacuate wounded soldiers. One New Zealand soldier, affectionately known as "the donkey man," returned the favor by rescuing and adopting "Roly" during the British campaign in Turkey.[1]

Tens of thousands of people have rescued them in other ways, some by creating sanctuaries for donkeys and mules destined for the slaughterhouse. After the conclusion of this book, we list some of the donkey sanctuaries around the world. Places of peace where donkeys—saved from years of maltreatment—are given the oases they deserve, so that they may live out their lives to forty, fifty, even sixty years in blessed surroundings. And where, in some instances, people of all ages can visit them and fall swoon to their charms. Such love affairs, we have discovered, are inevitable.

In 1956, Juan Ramon Jimenez received the Nobel Prize for Literature. This enormously sophisticated artist had achieved his most memorable fame with his book, *Platero y yo*, written in 1914, a year before the Battle of Gallipoli. Platero was a donkey who spent his years with a poet in and around a village in Andalusia. The poet and Platero are, for lack of a better description, at one with each other. The story is told in simple and enchanting prose. One might read *Platero y yo* as a primer on love,

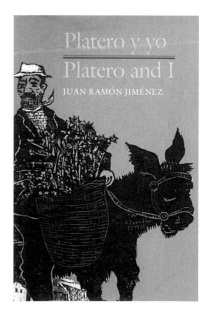

Platero y yo
Platero and I
JUAN RAMÓN JIMÉNEZ

compassion and character. It is about the human need for friendship exemplified by one little donkey and the truth of his unending emotional and imaginative life. The poet, Jimenez, claimed the Nobel Prize and Platero took his place in readers' hearts and walked into the donkey Hall of Fame.

Recent DNA and archaeological evidence suggests that asses, or donkeys if you prefer, are indigenous to parts of Africa. There appear to be two sub-species in Africa, *Equus asinus somaliensis* and *africanus*. It is difficult to know how many wild ones are left (one estimate suggests fewer than six hundred), especially in light of the more than six thousand years of documented domestication across the rural continent.[2] Worldwide, there are estimated to be approximately forty-four million donkeys at present and perhaps as many as sixty-five million horses, *Equus caballus*, the vast majority of whom are "maintained for work."[3] In fact, in terms of weight loads, some donkeys have been forced to carry nearly the same weight borne by elephants. The mules' alleged capacity for

strength and endurance has been their torment; that and the belief that donkeys and mules can survive with less food, can be forced to work harder for more hours, can run faster, can maintain better health and can live longer than their relative the horse.

We have spent time with donkeys in Mexico and India, in Greece and regions of Africa, throughout Europe, England and parts of South America and Central Asia, and have witnessed the abuse of these gentle creatures, usually for "traction," the hauling of heavy loads for impoverished families, as among the more than five million donkeys in Ethiopia and 1.6 million in India. Yet, everywhere, even under the most horrible of circumstances, the souls of donkeys speak when spoken to, grateful for the slightest gesture of sincerity and kindness. Their eyes sparkle; they smile; they verbalize in whole paragraphs, operas-worth of discourse. We hear of "horse whisperers." But among donkeys and mules, it would require more than a familiar sensitivity, we believe, to gain access to the inner circle of donkey trust. In that respect, they re-

mind us of tigers, grizzly bears and great white sharks. Some mysteries may be better left pure with dreams unanalyzed.

The donkeys maintain a poignant conversation. It doesn't matter what science calls it, we hear conversation, meandering rhythms, rhyme schemes, rich gossip, every cadence of tandem expressiveness. Record their myriad brays, play them back at half-speed, and the otherwise inaudible layers of nuance and verbal facility begin to announce their rich vocabularies and a range of expressive enunciations. They may wield more verb tenses than we can imagine. And, as with birds and cows, they may likely speak with regional dialects or accents.

Donkeys form lasting bonds like nearly every species. When one of them is losing his or her eyesight, typically, another will become the special friend, a seeing-eye. Their joy is always there; they are ready to bray, to inquire, to meet the moment. While their teeth are sharp, to be sure, they will explore new food and objects with their enormous, ever so delicate lips. We have just seen one donkey friend lick the arm of a gentle giant of a contractor consulting on barn repairs.

That lick, which is a kiss, reminds us of a pair of miniature donkey companions, little Barnie and the much bigger Little Ricky. With their large heads and sturdy though small bodies, these di-

A FARMER AND HIS DONKEY WORKING IN A VINEYARD
JOHN HOLMWOOD, 1910–1987

minutive equines are impressive and picturesque. Little Ricky is a piggle-puss. When he finishes his special meal, he noses Barnie aside and raids his friend's food, clearly indicating who is the alpha donkey in this group of two. But, Little Ricky has a soft side; he loves to give kisses. In fact, while Barnie remains aloof, Little Ricky lavishes licks upon those who draw near him. Still, one cannot impose upon this loving spirit. He and Barnie share this independence with their donkey brethren.

A man cannot force donkeys to do anything, except at the price of his own self-esteem and humanity. If anything, it was the don-

FLIGHT INTO EGYPT, GIOTTO DI BODONE, 1266–1336

key's profound dignity as well as lovingness that Jimenez observed
and revealed to grateful readers of all ages.

A donkey carried Christ into Jerusalem. Another bore Mary
and the Holy Family on their legendary flight into Egypt. These
are two of the great artistic themes of the Renaissance, as is the
depiction of a donkey in nearly every nativity scene. One of countless images throughout the world is a brilliant medieval sculpture

NATIVITY, FRA DIAMANTE, 1430–1498

at the Cathedral of Chartres of Christ riding a smiling donkey. The collection at Cluny in Paris has a wood and polychrome processional figure of Christ astride a grinning, uncannily knowing donkey on wheels.

The donkey appears nearly everywhere there is great art and literature. From the Eastern Desert rock art in ancient Egypt, to the Bible, Aesop and Shakespeare, the donkey makes much more than

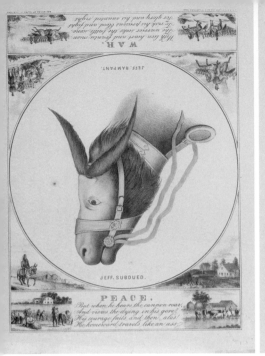

PEACE/WAR. PUBLISHED BY E.B. AND E.C. KELLOGG, 1861–1863

an occasional splash or odd cameo appearance. Rather, the donkey
has long been a major motif in history, biogeography, ecology, politics, aesthetics and religion. The donkey was used by Andrew Jack-
son's opponents in the 1830s to characterize him for his views, but
he turned this to his political advantage and the donkey became
the mascot of the Democratic Party. In the 1860s, the donkey appeared in political cartoons representing the Confederacy and Jef-
ferson Davis.

For many poor families throughout the world, the donkey is a
friend and salvation. And while there is no way to be sure just how
reciprocal the relationship, the donkey is a source of perpetual
spring, a living treasure inhabiting his and her own Eden, a being
who is honest, forthright, compassionate and loving. The donkey

JEFF. SEES THE ELEPHANT.

POLITICAL CARTOON. PUBLISHED BY E.B. AND E.C. KELLOGG, 1861–1863

is a creature whose observations of and insights into the world, we can only imagine.

In their translated selections from *Platero and I*, Myra Cohn Livingston and Joseph F. Dominguez write of Platero "looking up to the stars with tenderness, with his own unquenchable yearning. . . ."[4] This is the metaphysical donkey whose spirit we hope to convey. These donkeys are timeless. To us their smiles lend hope to the world; their eyes give meaning and solace to emptiness; their bursts of enthusiasm counter darkness with light; and their curiosity defines "endless."

Those familiar with them know that donkeys speak about them at night, remember them, look to them, would journey with them if the bond could be trusted. That bond is not just

{49}

PLAYMATES. *THE BURRO BOOK*, 1900

about getting a carrot. The human relationship with donkeys is about poetry and enchantment, about inner feelings and the sharing of all things unknown. The science of deep ethology—of spiritual interspecies communication—is this communal hope. The wilderness is in their eyes, the wilderness we cherish and safeguard. In their hearts is the most pure and idealistic region on Earth.

We do not presume to know much about donkeys. And this book is nothing more than a gesture of gratitude to them for having let us wander, at times, among their community of poets, prophets, clowns and minstrels.

On a Winter's Morning

*I*t is a cold winter morning somewhere in the coastal mountains of California. Emerging from the mist is a magnificent herd of donkeys. They are "partly" wild. That is to say, they are rescued animals that still retain their wild genes, if you will. Accustomed to a few people, with whom they associate food, treats, grooming, veterinary necessities and sheer fun, they look at us and are instantly curious, as are we. There are no donkey foals. The animals have all been "fixed." Normally, this time of year would see numerous jennets being tailed by their not-yet-weaned single offspring or, on rare occasions, twins. Such young would then achieve puberty within twelve to twenty-four months, as with horses.

Several dozen donkeys mosey along a grassy verge. Some graze. Enriched grass, almost "hot" in protein—due to all of the recent rains—is always an issue for donkeys. The consumption of too much high-protein grass can result in a metabolic ailment known as hyperlipaemia. Moreover, pasture feed must have plentiful mineral content, such as zinc and selenium. Donkeys seem to know the best foraging grounds, contrary to the common opinion that they'll eat anything.[1] This terrain is not unlike that which can be found throughout much of California's mountainous systems, between the ocean and the Central Valley, namely, a region of native species like bunch grass and non-natives including the bedeviling foxtails and wild oats. One finds here mixed broom, meadow grass, legumes and timothy, in addition to countless weeds—both native and exotic—shrubs, herbs, clovers, nuts and berries. History has not been entirely kind to native California ecosystems.

The same, sadly, can be said of introduced mammals, like donkeys. Wild ones are rare in the state. And, sanctuaries for donkeys are few and far between. These donkeys obtain shelter and soul satisfaction from a lush forest providing the shade from several oak species, a woodland forest under-story, chaparral and sage scrub. There is also a creek, teeming with *Toxicodendron diversilobum*, one of the most fearsome of Latin names, because it refers to poison oak, to which donkeys are apparently immune. There are four species of glorious manzanita, arroyo willows, California coffee-berry,

Bay trees, creeping snowberry and the glossy green smooth orange-trunked Madrones. The wildlife that joins the donkeys in their daily and nightly sojourns includes such creatures as Merriam chipmunks, western rattlesnakes, brown creepers, acorn woodpeckers, California voles, northern flickers, western waxwings, Cooper's hawks, American kestrels, garter snakes, deer mice, Yellow-billed magpies, wren-tits, winter wrens, mountain quail and a variety of lizards, like the western whiptail.

All in all, it is a busy, noisy, remarkable canopy. These donkeys inhabit a world where hundreds of wild turkeys and numerous white-tail deer mingle with them on a daily basis, where bobcats and an occasional mountain lion roam. And where, no doubt, human eyes are yet to encounter new species. Here is the unknown, the unexamined and truly wild. This seems to enter into the subconscious of every creature, human or otherwise, who ventures here.

This is an abundant forest that provides a safe haven for these large ungulates. No matter from where they've come, the reality today is that they are here, they are wanted and wonderful, and they remain a mystery to us.

Floppy exemplifies this wondrous, tentative, will-be relationship. Floppy is a wild child whose right ear flops forward. He seems a loner but harbors huge curiosity about humans. Clearly, he yearns to come to us but doesn't trust being in close proximity. Given human history's pattern of domination and abuse, his cautions may be in his genes or deep memory. While we may believe it in the worst interest of wild things to trust humans, our wish is that Floppy knows he may trust us.

The desire to share the joy of experiencing donkeys with other people is a bit like trying to describe the evanescent glint of light dancing on a creek at sunrise, or a Chopin nocturne quietly seducing us to sleep, or the sensation of first falling in love. That mystery is not necessarily penetrated by the myriad poetic tales about donkeys; a literature that abounds with names and giant personalities, like *Brighty of the Grand Canyon*, "Blizzard," or "Naughty Face," the first donkey rescued by Elisabeth Svendsen in the United Kingdom in 1969.[2] In reviewing that literature, what is especially curious to contemplate, when standing among donkeys on such a particularly wild winter morning, is the degree to which the countless writers on this species have been moved either toward their own childhood,

or toward humor, cuteness or some religious bliss. Note titles like *Donkeys Can't Sleep in Bathtubs, Sweetly Sings the Donkey, The Donkey of Nazareth, A Foolish Miller and His Donkey, Pin the Tail on the Donkey and Other Party Games, Little Donkey: The Story of the First Christmas, Dancing With Mules* and *Please, God, Take Care of the Mule.* And, of course, there is Eeyore who continues to captivate children and adults alike with his resolute resignation. [3]

But back to these particular donkeys on this particular morning: in their presence we feel humility, rapture, wonder. They are koans, Zen riddles that require some exploration and patience. Patience because, initially, on this day, the donkeys have their own agenda and we stand isolated, outsiders looking in.

As we gaze upon their meandering presences, we see faintly outlined against the dense forest vestiges of that prehistoric time when these odd-toed creatures were not far removed from the last of the dinosaurs and stood a mere half a foot tall: "the dawn horse" or eohippus. Scientific words—describing many of the different and now extinct horse groups such as Propalaeotherium and Hyracotherium, et cetera[4]—are no less alien than the contemporary tags employed to somehow get the scientific, or hybridized, names of the living ones right.

It is argued that 99.9 percent of all species on Earth (perhaps as many as fifty billion throughout time) have gone extinct. But these donkeys seem absolutely steadfast. Of course, so did *Tyrannosaurus rex*. So do the elephant, the blue whale and the redwood. If the meek do, in fact, inherit the Earth, then donkeys are somewhere between the tiny mammalian mouse shrew, the wild grass

species, and birds—all of which have survived so well over time—
and those other huge charismatic megaflora and fauna mentioned
above which have grown enormous, and powerful, but are hugely
vulnerable. Donkeys combine the best character traits of both ex-
tremes, it would seem, but they don't need to flaunt them. Content
within their own mysterious worlds, they seem socially at ease
and marvelously adapted. We envy them. We love them. And we
suspect and hope that they love us, as well.

BLACKIE AND MOHAWK

Blackie and Smiley are rivals for Michael's attention. They ramble under the sycamores and oaks until Michael draws near, then they act as bookends, in affectionate embrace of their human friend and smile at the camera. Actually, Smiley grins. They both give Michael kisses and sniff his otherness with interest and unabashed affection.

Blackie and Mohawk investigate each other cautiously. After expressing mutual curiosity with a neck-reaching Eskimo kiss, they resume grazing. Blackie is a leaner whose head often rests on one of our shoulders or pushes against our backs. He loves the proximity, pressure and a good mane scratch.

Donkeys have been forced into nearly every environment, from the Himalayas to the Sahara Desert. They have bolstered their vulnerability by developing the most powerful of all "gaskins"—that disproportionately large muscle in their hind legs, above the hock (the heel). And their thiry-six to forty teeth grow extremely sharp with the years as they grind their food like well-tuned engines.

▲ Deep in conversation   ▼ Blackie, Michael and Smiley

They can live in excess of sixty years. This is worth keeping in mind when you consider that in some parts of Africa the human life expectancy is well below fifty. In feral terms, with feral being defined as independent, geographically separated and self-sustaining populations that once were wild and appear to be so again, donkey sociology is similar to that of horses. A hyena or lion might try to kill them in Africa, but elsewhere their only predators are bacteria, viruses, drought, brushfires and, primarily, humans. Those same humans who have, over time, thought of them in religious terms, painted them as exquisite embodiments of tenderness and formed bonds with them for one reason or other, as well as exploited them.

We love donkeys, and in the donkey world, they certainly love each other. Among horses, one dominant male is likely to stir up the continuing interest of up to three mares. But, as scientist Sue

M. McDonnell has researched, the sexual relations among donkeys are somewhat different from the "harem system typical of horses and some zebras," and represent a "more stable affiliation" between those male and female donkeys who are sexually active. It can mean more partners for the male donkey but a more sedate territorial rule, sometimes in the company of "subordinate males" who might breed (make love) or not.[5] Female donkeys (jennies) take a very active role in sexual activities, putting what appears to be considerable energy into the stimulation of male partners.[6] In studies among zebras and feral asses in Africa, as well as on the Volcano Alcedo in the Galapagos Islands of Ecuador, a "female (harem) defense polygynous mating system" has been reported.[7] This means that the territorial distribution and breeding success of the female donkeys is expedited by their joining harems of particularly virile males, males who can protect them and support the territorial dispersion females require.

TENDING THE FLOCKS, *BURRO WITH FOAL* BY THOMAS SIDNEY COOPER

The reason there are fewer male donkeys available for mating is the factor of their intra-gender competition for the females (same old story). Hence, there is little likelihood of much monogamy among them. In such systems, younger males spend time together in so-called bachelor groups.[8] Underscoring the donkey's incredible adaptability, sexual maturity occurs within two years, and oftentimes sooner.[9] Females gestate (like cows) for twelve months (some up to fourteen months). Horses gestate for eleven. That means that when baby donkeys are born (feet first), they are ready to get going. They are curious. Already wondering what's for dinner. And, they appear far more evolved as donkeys, than those organisms, like humans, that only get, say, nine months in the womb, give or take.

There is a strongly-held belief by many that donkeys are more self-preserving, or "intelligent," if you will, than their close cousins, horses. One reason for this assumption is that they do not flee with the skittishness of horses, but, rather, stand their ground, examining the situation. There are numerous theories about the evolutionary behavior of donkeys: issues of genetic drift from other equines and the proliferation of breeds over time. Donkeys seem to have acquired new traits with the appearance of human beings in their lives. For example, they have been used by some sheep herders to protect their flocks from predators, bears or big cats; and have also been used by ranchers to "cut" or select out certain other equines for breeding or segregation purposes.

Donkeys are no threat to large horses. The small hinney, Mikey, is best friends with an enormous Arabian stallion named Super 8. The gorgeously golden draught horse Nazarene has as his pal the tiny donkey Doobie. These two loving odd couples stick to one another's sides, as best friends, though temporary companions. When the horses are let out into the herd, the donkeys may not be able to keep up their pace if they are very old. Then they will have to cast about for new companions.

HERCULES AND HENRIETTA

We gaze upon a herd of donkeys on this winter morning and realize that we can read anything we want into them, or not. Shall we wait instead for a surprise or, perhaps, instruction? They upend our every assumption. We stand curious, mesmerized and enchanted, gazing at a wonder of creation. It is the beginning of a relationship.

Approaching a Donkey

TAKE ONE ON ME.

hen approaching donkeys, the first, most overwhelming sensation is that they do not seem menacing. They will not chase us down and eat us, or kick us to death. They are gentle though not without "personality." Their ancestry is as exotic as Mountain Zebras from East Africa, to whom they are related. It is said that donkeys are hearty, able to withstand harsh temperatures, go long periods without water and carry huge loads. This characterization we find inappropriate. Whether a person, by analogy, can suffer for months, is no indicator of whether that person would prefer to suffer for months. Nowhere in the equation of arid lands are donkeys supposed to be. They manage only because they have no other choice. We forced them into this dilemma.

Curiously, the biology of donkeys may not be very different from that of humans. The DNA and taxonomic structure of donkeys incorporates a long biological history—a social network fifty-million-years old combining traits that are shared at nearly every phylogenetic level with humans: Kingdom, Animala, Phylum, Chordata, Sub-phylum, Vertebrata, Class, Mammalian Eutherials—placental, in other words. We then separate slightly at the Order level, wherein donkeys go the way of Perissodactyla (non-ruminant ungulates with an odd number of toes per foot), the Family Equidae, Genus *Equus* (asses, horses and zebras).[1]

The belief that donkeys may have originated as domesticated ungulates in Northeastern Africa, in harsh, desert environments, in other words, fails to recognize that domestication may have had

nothing to do with the donkey's preference or geographical origins. The fact that African caravans subjected donkeys to the servitude that has become their legendary cross to bear, not just across Africa but from Malta to England, from India to Brazil, for century upon century, is no reliable indicator of what donkeys actually are best at doing.[2]

What we believe *Equus asinus* most prefers is simply to be left alone so that they may graze casually, marvel at their surroundings, meditate on other life forms, drink plenty of water, have fun, sing, sleep, make love, raise their young, have parties and discuss the great issues of life. In a study in West Africa the observation of donkeys' natural behavior revealed sixteen separate activities, of which eighty-five percent among adults and sixty-two percent for the young (foals) involved grazing. Foals spent more time grooming.[3] But, human observation does not account for our inability to recognize other possible activities (acoustical, psychic, emotive) occurring simultaneously with what we term "grazing" and "grooming". Indeed, studies that have compared feral donkeys in the Northern Panamint Range of Death Valley with a population on Ossabaw Island, Georgia, as well as on the Caribbean island of St. John and in the Danakil Desert of Ethiopia, reveal a more refined sense of a complex social structure at work; more "social play," "mutual grooming" as well as "five types of vocalizations," namely, "brays, grunts, growls, snorts and whuffles."[4] In the case of the St. John herd, "eighteen grouping patterns (social units) were observed."[5] Donkeys are such social, herd beings, that some

AFFECTION.

breeders refuse to sell just one donkey, insisting the donkey must have a companion.

One careful observer has noted four donkey postures that might explain volumes' worth in terms of body language: "Yes, No, What and Fear." The way Vicki Knotts Abbott has translated these expressions, at least for "Yes," is as follows: She writes, "When a donkey raises his head on an upright neck so his eye is above his withers, swivels his ears forward, and has an expectant expression, he is asking a question. What? Huh? Why? Hello? Is it time for supper? Do you have any cookies?" et cetera.[6]

But what's really going on might be something else. We think Abbott is probably correct. But we have also experienced contradictions to "Yes," variations on "Huh?" and distinct uncertainties with respect to "Fear." We can't say for certain, but it would seem that animals of any degree of wildness (or reversion to semi-wildness when provided sanctuary and relative freedom), ones favored with affection and non-interference, are more likely to be sociable and agreeable when approached.

Donkeys appear to have no such ambivalence when it comes to their own moral superiority. They appear both to love their neighbors and do not kill, though will rally in defense of the flocks, or individuals, they frequently shepherd. They are open, honest and inquisitive. They approach us, just as we approach them. Whatever bad blood may exist between humans and donkeys, they are a study, this day, in total forgiveness, unconditional love and all of those characteristics which flood the spiritual libraries and great classics of the human species.

How is it that animals are so loving and patient with us when we as a species have been so outrageously inconsistent in our behavior towards them? One thing is certain: more and more people are falling in love with equines, and donkeys particularly, because there is an innate bond that seems to have come of age, primeval chimes of mutual recognition.

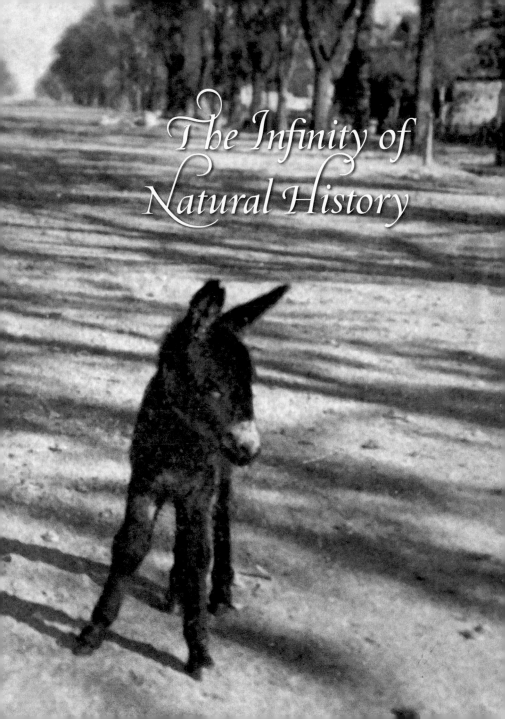

The Infinity of
Natural History

*D*onkeys have found their habitat dwindle generation after generation. Wild equines in North America are rare because their habitat has been so continuously squeezed, fenced in and diminished. In order to better grasp the scope of their habitat fragmentation, consider two other species that shared North America with them, and whose populations in the wild have been utterly transformed: pronghorn antelope and bison, both numbering well over fifty million two hundred years ago, today reduced by more than ninety-nine percent. Hence, human contact with donkeys has built-in biases: the animals may be hungry or thirsty, or riddled with parasites and look to humans, possibly, as a source of assistance even at the price of their freedom. The impact by humans might even explain why some donkeys develop "esophageal obstruction," as a result of masticating their food too fast, "without sufficient chewing."[1]

That survival trade-off is not an intangible. The donkey is a large, intelligent mammal who knows what is happening and makes decisions based upon survival needs. That is fundamental to all organisms, but especially so when there is distinct pleasure and a survival component involved, such as a good meal or fresh water. This inclination on the part of the donkey may have been passed down from generation to generation. It certainly has among people.

Wild donkeys are believed to vary from ten to fourteen hands in height (one hand being equal to 10.2 centimeters, or approximately four inches) as measured from their withers. The grandest

MULE

ZEBRA

DONKEY

2.

QUAGGA

of donkeys may be twenty percent larger than that, while adult weights vary from approximately 250 pounds to as much as 1,700 pounds.[2]

It is assumed that donkeys and mules managed, somehow miraculously, to outsmart their own vulnerability, that they are smarter and appear less likely to be injured, or to suffer, than are horses. This is why, according to John Hauer in his delightful article "The Natural Superiority Of The Mule," the Navajo Indians supposedly considered the price of one mule to be equivalent to that of two horses.[3] This mindset was fortified by a famous race involving General George Custer on his horse and Bill Cody on a mule. Over harsh terrain and long distance, Custer's horse died, over-ridden, while Cody's mule survived the endurance race to win.[4] Mules are fast, faster usually than horses. And they can leap over deer fences, which exceed six feet in height. If you've heard a donkey bray up close, you know they are not shy about conveying anxiety, excitement, enthusiasm, loneliness or anything else they wish verbally to express. Cloned donkeys recently lost a forced race against horses.

Donkeys experience huge anticipation, which can be about worry or gladness. They must wonder why humans have continued to trade, purchase and sell them, removing them from friends, family and familiar landscapes; where they are trucked off, experimented on, overburdened and too often slaughtered. These traumas and emotions may inform the consciousness of the modern donkey, mentor the mule and embroider their imaginations. When Lewis and Clark were buying horses and mules from Indians during their travels, they always paid more for the *Equus asinus*, whether

from the Flathead or Shoshone. One mule cost "2 knives, a shirt, 2 handkerchieves, and a pair of leggings." Native Americans maintained varying attitudes towards donkeys, mules and horses. The Mandans, for example, never ate any equine so far as we are aware, whereas the Chiracauha Apaches were said to have preferred mule meat over any other dish.[5]

Much of a donkey's pain is suffered silently, with inner-resolve that seems a mark of their character. Donkeys and mules are lionized for their strength, wit and inner-knowledge, but are rarely re-paid by humans for these prized qualities. However, when President Abraham Lincoln heard that Civil War rebels had captured

an army general along with forty mules the news reported that he said, "I'm sorry to lose those mules."[6]

Donkeys don't over-drink water in the heat, or walk backwards off cliffs or run through fences. Their large ears are good for listening to the universe and also emanate heat which helps them maintain thermal homeostatsis. With ears serving as enormous antennae, they have the advantage over most creatures by being tuned in to the music of the spheres. They hear everything. This capacity is beautifully represented by one of the greatest Italian painters of the fifteenth century, Piero Della Francesca who, in a Nativity painting, depicts a donkey singing at the very center of the composition as angels strum heavenly music in celebration of the infant Jesus' birth. This delightful image hangs in London's

National Gallery. We sometimes play classical music for donkeys and they appear to be drawn toward it and to enjoy it.

In spite of this glorious legacy of strength, legendary durability, acute sensory apparatuses and any number of other attributes, including the fact that males are vastly endowed, the list of potential medical issues for donkeys and mules is sadly long: from an uncommon propensity for respiratory problems,[7] to discharges from their eyes, abscesses, the impacting of sand in their intestines which leads to colic, mites in their ears, rain scald (resulting from continuously wet skin and hair), foot scald (also known as inter-digital dermatitis, which comes about under conditions of sustained moisture on the hooves) and a variety of arthritic pains.[8] While a donkey's feet are thought of as "bare," their hooves cracking less frequently than those of horses, they have other problems. Donkeys can be poisoned by certain plants like ragwort, and, in some cases, if the grass or cereals on which they feed are extremely high in carbohydrates, and they consume abundant amounts of it, the supply of blood to their feet can be altered, causing inflammation of the laminae that hold the bone to the hooves. This is called laminitis or foundering and is terribly painful. It can even be lethal.[9]

Moreover, older donkeys are susceptible to at least three known types of sarcoids, or connective tissue tumors formed by a virus. These tumors can grow to the size of an orange and then ulcerate, causing life-threatening infections. Donkeys also may develop carcinomas, as well as melanomas. The iris around the pupil can become inflamed for a number of reasons, including trauma; they can go blind, die of worms or succumb to influenza virus or

tetanus. Donkeys can also spread glanders, a bacterial disease, to humans. If it is untreated in donkeys, they cough, discharge through the nose, suffer swollen lymph glands and high fever and can die within two weeks. [10]

In one study across Botswana, investigators discovered that the major diseases affecting donkeys there were rabies, babesiosis (a protozoan infection caused by ticks), dourin (a protozoan parasite known as *Trypanosoma equiperdum* that affects the nervous system following intercourse) and strongylosis (a parasitic nematode, much like the hookworm, that can infest the donkey's intestines).[11] In Nigeria, a large number of donkeys contract tuberculosis.

Scientists have looked at donkey physiology both with an eye towards their diseases, but also in terms of what uniquely gives donkeys their pertinacity and strength. In Israel, where the Black Bedouin Goat, the Nubian Ibex and the Donkey have each played a role in human societies for thousands of years, topics of particular interest and study have included metabolism, renal functions, re-hydration mechanisms, and other comparative physiological attributes, all of which show unique characteristics, particularly amongst donkeys.[12]

But, as stated above, these mythic mammals—seemingly able to endure all hardship—turn out to be exceedingly vulnerable, just like the rest of us. The famed eighteenth century naturalist Gilbert White observed this to be so as did the great poets William Word-

sworth in "Peter Bell" and Samuel Taylor Coleridge in "To a Young
Ass." Donkeys wake up with headaches, their teeth grow unevenly,
pushing persistently through the gums, and they can drop dead on
a dime if they're not careful or if life is unfair to them. Whoever
started the rumor that they are invulnerable clearly did so self-in-
terestedly in order to ignore their needs and woes and exploit them.
That ignorance is likely to be the most disturbing bias that one has
to contend with when approaching donkeys; they know that they
have been abused either in this life or some other. They remember
and recall instinctively, we believe, all of the donkey refugees and
victims in their family tree and their collective hardships.

There are widely varying opinions within the ecological and animal protection worlds with respect to how close one should ever
get to a wild animal. With donkeys, there is additional confusion,
depending upon whether a donkey is wild, feral or domestic. And
if domestic, what that means. None of these categories ultimately
matter, if the underlying concern is whether or not to make the
approach in the first place. The question of whether to ever touch
a wild animal, and if not, the degree of significance that should be
placed on the domestication factor, is important.

The domestication issue is particularly troubling with respect
to donkeys of whom G.K. Chesterton referred in his poem "The
Donkey" as "the tattered outlaw of the earth," because there are,
in fact, a number of breeds and varying types of so-called "conformation." The breeding of donkeys has often been done to produce
sterile mules, who have sixty-three sets of chromosomes whereas
horses have sixty-four, donkeys sixty-two. These mules will work—
as myth has it—forever, in any condition.

Donkeys can be distinguished by their markings, size, color and any number of other characteristics and are particularly well-delineated between the so-called Small and Large American Standard, the Mammoth Jack, Anatolian, Mary or Maryiskaya (in Turkmenia), the Abyssinian or Ethiopian, the Baudet de Poitou in France (highly endangered), the miniatures from several Mediterranean islands, and—in Spain—five different known breeds.[13]

In the Near East, other possible breeds may be discerned. The Emirate of Sharja has its own resident donkey type, *Equus africanus f. asinus*, found in the Dhaid-al-Madam plain.[14] And, in Muscat and Yemen on the splendid Island of Soqotra, there is another endemic ass which is said to possibly harbor a genetic link

UNTITLED, CHARLES F. LUMMIS

to the oldest wild asses in the world. In the Kutch of Gujarat, in northwestern India, there is yet another breed called the Khur. In the U.S., it is the "pinto" or American spotted ass, the wild burros, and a long-time breeding mule group unique to Mexico, all of whom finally gained recognition of their rarity with passage of *The Wild Free-Roaming Horses and Burro Act of 1971*. Despite repeated attempts to undo the protections afforded by the Act, it was reaffirmed unanimously in the House of Representatives on May 18, 2006, with the passage of an amendment prohibiting taxpayer funds from being used to sell or slaughter America's free-roaming horses and burros.[15]

There are still other hybrid forms as recorded by the American Donkey and Mule Society.[16] Registries include the racing mules, the miniatures, the standards and the mammoths.[17] Among the zebra/male donkey offspring are four listed crosses, namely, the "zonkey, zebroid, zebras, or zedonk." The zebra/female donkey young are called "zebra hinny, zebret, and zebrinny."[18]

Zebras have forty-four chromosomes sets, roughly thirty percent fewer than donkeys. Yet, their hybrids can survive, with still other generic names used in various parts of the world such as zebra mule, deebra, zenkey, zebadonk, zorse, zoney, zenkey and other odd combinations. Haldane's Rule is the genetic model of probability used to describe sterility among male hybrids. Yet, there are rare instances where the hybridized male offspring will not be sterile.

Words for these creatures proliferate, as do their markings, intermingled genetics, deep lineages and sobriquets. Jennet, mule, hinny, Spanish Jack, mare, foal, produce, stud, dames, sires, gelding donkeys and wild burros are but a few points of a vast pointillist canvas. Donkey parlance is further complicated by breeders who lavish affection on these equines with the authority, single-mindedness and kin-altruism of grandparents naming and indulging their grandchildren. Donkey lovers are, in fact, a fantastic breed of their own, and we have the highest admiration for their passion and love though would never condone breeding for purposes of any form of exploitation,

{62}

ZEBRA. COMTE DE BUFFON, 1839

By far the most intensive examination of the donkey taxonomy was undertaken by Colin P. Groves who proposed the concept of para-species to differentiate wild from domestic, suggesting degrees of difference. Ernst Mayr, the Harvard evolutionary biologist suggested a rule of thumb whereby if seventy-five percent of individuals look different from another group, they would qualify as a sub-species. Sympatric individuals—those occupying the same geographical region, but not breeding; and allopatric species—those occupying different geographical regions—make for additional complications. Groves concludes, "The wild species may have subspecies; the domestic species does not."[19]

On the British Isle of Guernsey, locals are sometimes referred to by outsiders as "donkeys." And those who speak with the local dialect of the town of Castel are "ane-pur-sangs, or, pure-blooded-donkeys." One writer living on Guernsey says, "...we're proud to be a donkey first and a European second."[20] The Butterflat Farm website points out that a stockbroker named Robert Green fell in love with Sardinian Miniature donkeys during the Depression years and ultimately found himself surrounded by some fifty of these fabulous companions. He is quoted as saying that they had "the courage of a tiger and the intellectual capability only slightly inferior to a man's."[21]

Juliet Clutton-Brock concludes her study of equines by acknowledging that "the family Equidae is unusual amongst mammals in that all of the species of horse, ass, onager, and zebra can interbreed and will produce hybrid offspring."[22] This capacity places the taxonomic donkey in a remarkable setting, considering the eighteen known wild equine species, eight of which have gone extinct. Those diverse creatures—from Somalia to Ireland, from Central Asia to South America—included the Tarpan (a now extinct Eurasian wild horse), wild asses in Algeria, Mongolia, Tibet and southern Europe; the extinct Quagga, the Mountain Zebra, the Nubian and Somali wild asses and all of the horse, donkey and mule breeds that make up the domestic ass/donkey and horse—more than 220 equine breeds worldwide. The diversity of their forms and the fact of their ability to breed with one another, combined with a unique capacity to survive so many different environments give *Equus* a paramount place in biology. But their genius for diffusion and distribution must be tempered by the sad truth that the vast majority of them have gone extinct since the original divergence of Hipparion from Dinohippus tens of millions of years ago in North America. The former line of equids went ex-

tinct, whilst Dinohippus, according to Clutton-Brock, trotted to Asia and evolved into *Equus ferus*—the first truly wild horse.[23]

In the first week of May 2006, the IUCN (the International Union for the Conservation of Nature and Natural resources, or World Conservation Union, comprised of 10,000 scientists, 181 signatory nations and 800 NGOs) held a global conference in Geneva, Switzerland, and scientists predicted that by the end of the twenty-first century, another sixteen thousand species might well go extinct, including polar bears, hippos, desert gazelles, one in eight bird species, a large number of coniferous and palm trees, a third of all amphibians, all of the large fish in the seas, most charismatic megafauna and equines. In the context of this sixth spasm of extinctions in the history of life on Earth, various equid researchers are attempting to revivify the various equine genetic

ONAGERS

palettes with living individuals so as to provide for their ultimate survival.

The Quagga Project, as summarized by renowned naturalist Richard Ellis, is one such undertaking that grew out of impassioned efforts by Dr. J. F. Warning, a veterinarian, and his colleagues at the South African Museum. The quagga was related to the plains zebra. The last one in the wild was evidently shot in 1878. Five years later the final remaining captive quagga perished in an Amsterdam zoo. Today, the Quagga Project's selective breeding program with plains zebras has resulted in six distinct populations in Africa that, with each passing generation, are looking more and more like quaggas.[24]

Similarly, the Przewalski's wild horse has been saved from extinction through systematic efforts to breed them for over a century. The last sighting of these gorgeous horses in the wild occurred at a spring in Southwestern Mongolia. Today, the Foundation for the Preservation and Protection of the Przewalski Horse—working with other organizations—has managed to return dozens of Przewalskis into large Mongolian preserves, and the fertility rate among the mares has exceeded ninety percent. Other Przewalskis have been returned to their traditional range, the Dzungarian desert in China.[25]

QUAGGA

Such breeding efforts and reintroductions should give equine lovers some cause for optimism. The very latitude built into the equids' deep genetic lineage will prove to be their salvation to the extent that information and passion are leveraged for advocacy. But there will be continuing issues to work through. In Australia, for example, there are an estimated 300,000 feral horses (the first horse was introduced on that Continent in 1788). And, there are as many as five million feral donkeys largely inhabiting "central Australia, the Kimberley in Western Australia and the Top End in the Northern Territory."[26] With both sets of populations, there has been an ongoing debate as to their ecological impact and the appropriate responses by the government and farmers. In South Africa a similar debate turned violent when donkeys were viewed as pests and, in 1983, twenty thousand of the equines in the Kuruman tribal area were killed.

A Transcendent Reality
Begins to Emerge

Le Baudet © La Poste

*T*he Greeks thought of the donkey as Dionysus, an orgiastic, wine-drinking party animal. In Egypt, the ass was said to look like Seth, the Egyptian Lord associated with sand storms. In either case, the donkey is a very wild creature.

Over time, repeated attempts have been made to breed that wildness out of donkeys. Take, for example, the case of the extremely endangered Poitou donkey in France, documented as early as the time of Christ, during the Roman occupation of Gaul, if not before. Today, fewer than 400 Poitou donkeys are left and that's because their function as breeders for mules fell out of vogue. Traditionally, they were bred with a horse known as the Mulassier to produce what was believed to be the hardest working mule in the world, the Poitou mule. They were among the 300,000 mules forced into battle against the Germans. Mules, in general, are fast. In the U.K., a donkey named Minstrel was purchased for his speed and put into races. Minstrel was sold for 25,000 pounds, a record in England.[1]

After World War II, mules were little in demand in France and many of the purebred Poitou donkeys were sent to slaughter, allegedly to provide food for the hungry French. Today the Poitou is an endangered breed whose future hangs on the inspired efforts of such donkey devotees as those at La Maison du Baudet du Poitou.[2] Other rare French donkeys were less equipped for purposes of guaranteeing hard-working offspring, namely, the Grand Noir du Berry Donkey and the Provence Donkey. Their coloring, size, conformation and habitat differ from those of the Poitou, but they share a gentleness. And they, too, have become rare.

TAKING A SAND BATH

As of 1970, mules, in general, were "nearing extinction," wrote Theodore Savory in a *Scientific American* article. According to a graph calculating their rate of decline, Savory suggested that the "complete extinction of mules in the U.S." was predicted by 1958. And while that grim prediction has not materialized, "the outcome is unmistakable," he declared. Of this fear, he concluded, ". . . they deserve a fate better than such an obscure drift toward oblivion."[3]

But whether speaking of the Poitou, or of the largest of all donkeys, the American Standard Jack or Mammoth, which towers a minimum of over fifty-six inches tall and weighs as much as a heavy draft horse, some 1,600 pounds—is it really possible to breed wildness out of an animal? And, do donkeys and mules differ in temperament as widely as is claimed by some?

It is believed that the Mammoth Jack derives from an accumulation of breeds from all known donkey types, other than the

Mediterranean miniatures, a complex, positively untraceable palette of bloodlines. In the U.S., mule breeding began when President George Washington was gifted two Spanish jacks, one named Royal Gift, whom he bred. Their female offspring were, in turn, mated with an Arabian horse, and that family tree has resulted in an animal frequently thought of as "the gentle giant," namely the largest of donkeys and mules in North America.[4]

The names became matters of some controversy and triggered enormous interest among scientists and breeders, spawning a range of classifications as early as 1758. That is when the Swedish botanist, Carolus Linnaeus published his 824-page *Systema Naturae*, in its tenth and most ambitious edition. This book defined 'species' and outlined a system of animal taxonomy that is known

54.

173

HORSE

as binomial, meaning it juxtaposed genus, species and sometimes sub-species. Thousands of "new" species have been discovered since his time, but the more than five hundred that Linnaeus identified remain largely uncontested as true species. His system—now ascribed to by most scientists—was debated feverishly in his day. In Linnaeus' time, philosophers like John Locke and biologists such as Georges-Louis Leclerc, Comte de Buffon (1707–1788) challenged him, assigning a host of varying definitions to what a species actually is and how to distinguish among them. Philosophers of the stature of Immanuel Kant, Diderot, Voltaire and Rousseau each strived to reveal the secret, inviolable laws governing nature.

We suspect that none of those great thinkers or scientists spent much time with donkeys, though Francois Marie Arouet de Voltaire fashioned an entire character, that of a philosopher, utilizing a donkey as his central figure and metaphor. His book, *The Ignorant Philosopher,* first published in English in 1767, revised the old myth of Plato's three blind men in a cave by creating three blind philosophers groping after a donkey. This, said Voltaire, was a fitting description of humanity's futile search for truth. He launched his tale by posing the essential questions: Who are we; where do we come from; what are we doing; and, what will become of us? The donkey epitomized for Voltaire the answer to all of these questions.

Buffon—whose thirty-six-volume *System of Nature* remains, along with Linnaeus' work, the most influential corpus of natural history—declared, "The ass resembles the horse more than the water spaniel the hound." But, he said, the latter can reproduce, whereas the former can only manage to create "defective and barren individuals."[5] This is not entirely true, but Buffon was not

A Rustic Couple in a Landscape with Two Donkeys and a Dog
Francois Boucher, ca. 1728

yet familiar with the statistical, albeit low, probability of fertiliza-
tion among mules. Buffon's "equids" were not the sweet, graceful,
godlike asses that Voltaire had enshrined. Hence, the metaphors
wielded by each man were a product of their individual biases.

Later, Buffon still struggled with asses and donkeys and, in his
essay "On the Degeneration of Animals," he acknowledged that
some mules might prove to be fertile after all, and he assigned the
"horse, zebra, ass and mule, fertile or infertile" to an Old World
genus he named solipeds, or "whole-hoofed animals."[6] In other
words, he bypassed the sexual issue completely, preferring to deal

with the group differently, to think (by his own standards) "outside of the box." In keeping with that creative breakthrough, Buffon declared that the ass "was a kind of horse."[7]

Such "kind of" remarks were important, he indicated, because "only through comparison do we know anything."[8] He had compared data from the sexual behavior of this group of solipeds when, in 1761, at the zoological assemblage known as the Menagerie at Versailles, keepers tried to mate a male zebra with various asses. The asses were all in heat. Buffon remarked that while the zebra played around with the girls, he could get no "erection" and Buffon took this as a sign that nature had arranged for an important biological barrier.[9]

The differences between science and literature, art and philosophy, turn out to be especially huge when it comes to the donkey.

Theodore Savory has come as close as anyone, we imagine, to describing—within the confines of a scientific journal—a beautiful ass, when he referred to mules, not as "defective" (as Buffon had called them) but as "sensitive spirits in robust bodies."[10]

Now let's take that belief a step further by looking at one of the most important literary works ever conceived and written, *The Life and Exploits of the Ingenious Gentleman Don Quixote de la Mancha*, by Miguel de Cervantes Saavedra (1547-1616). Part One was published in 1605 and Part Two, in 1615. It has been hailed as the "first modern novel" and also described as a novel wherein, for the first time in fiction, people actually listened to one another as opposed to simply spouting soliloquies. Indeed, in Cervantes, animals engage in dialogue rather than in allegorical speech, as can be read in the many renditions of the *Fables* of Aesop and Jean de La Fontaine.[11] Cervantes' animals speak not on behalf of a political or moral disposition, but as themselves. Their actions are described in a manner befitting their own nobility, weaknesses and strengths.

Don Quixote contains more than its engrossingly intimate, astonishingly lively *human* passion. It is one of the earliest epics in which animals serve as significant protagonists. Two of its four central characters are equines: Don Quixote's old horse, Rosinante and Sancho Panza's beloved donkey, Dapple. Without Rosinante and Dapple, there is no *Don Quixote*. In the book's globe-trotting satiric commentary, the great Don and his Squire require not just assistance or comic props to give them literary loft, but true companionship that mentors and delivers the unlikely heroes to their anointed roosts. Their two eternal equine companions are the mirrors of the men who ride them into every predicament and

SANCHO PANZA

AMSTERDAM

BOEK,-KUNST-& HANDELSDRUKKERIJ
V/H GEBR. BINGER.

misadventure. Whether it be battling giants who assume the form of windmills, taking a beating from liberated prisoners, falling swoon to one Dulcinea after another, disappearing in perilous canyons in the dark or venturing into wild, inhospitable mountain ranges: Rosinante and Dapple invariably carry the day.

Dapple's donkey diaries are a chronicle of Spain in the seventeenth century and of human companions who appear to be the sum total of so many lunacies, great dreams, lost loves and weeping hearts. Dapple endures, relishes, hopes, lives and dies at every turn of fortune, just as does Sancho Panza. It is the donkey and the horse that make the men who ride them. Without these two equine

SANCHO PANZA AND DAPPLE

friends, all the memorable battles, love affairs and outrageous adventures would lose much of their grip on posterity. Don Quixote rode into a celestial sphere on a swayback, used-up mare who loved him. And Dapple carried the simple Sancho Panza into a Spanish pantheon of myth, the most memorable tale ever told.

Note, for example, this description in Chapter 23 of Part One of Cervantes' epic, following Sancho Panza's discovery that he may have lost Dapple:

Aurora issued forth, giving joy to the earth, but grief to Sancho Panza who, when he missed his Dapple, began to utter
the most doleful lamentations, insomuch that Don Quixote awakened at his cries, and heard him say: "Oh child of
my bowels, born in my house, the joy of my children, the
entertainment of my wife, the envy of my neighbours, the
relief of my burdens, lastly, the half of my maintainance!"[2]

Consider the beginning of John Phillips' translation of *Don Quixote* (Phillips was John Milton's nephew and his translation of Cervantes' epic, the second English translation, was one of the first to
be illustrated). Prior to the Table of Contents, Phillips samples a
conversation between Dapple and Rosinante, wherein, says Dapple,
". . . the Poor themselves are Asses too, And love the Beasts that
carry as they do."

Rosinante, who wonders if she might therefore not be better

off with a Sancho Panza rather than with a worldly knight, replies, "How might I change? It is too late I fear." To which the wise donkey declares, "Not so, if thou an Asse's voice wilt hear. To England go, where Fools are rich in Purse, There give it out, thou art Don Quixote's Horse: Thou shalt be sought and bought, and taught to vault; Then shown at Fairs... Thus shalt thou live at ease..." and great bards shall write an elegy and a lamentation when she dies.[13]

HISTORIA NATURALIS, DE QUADRUPEDIBUS. JOHANN JONSTON, 1650–53

In his later *Fables*, Fontaine has two mules conversing. One carries a pricey load of silver, the other mere oats. Their respective destinies are charted when, while crossing through a wild forest, they are attacked by robbers and the thieves who, while trying to unburden the proud mule of his silver, are forced to kill him. In his dying throes, the mule laments the fact that this should be his reward for working so hard, only to be lectured by his oat-carrying companion who reminds him that one must never think too highly of one's self or one's station. Such moralizing distanced Fontaine from political censure. The earlier Cervantes—without drawing upon didactic allegory—storied the world with a stage of interacting protagonists, humans, donkeys, horses, et cetera, all who shared equally in the tragicomedy of life.

Great painters have also chosen to view donkeys as spiritual companions in an ethereal realm of life and death; the donkey equals man in the theatre of chance and is equally a part of that divine force in the universe. Consider the grand Emperor Napoleon hunkered down on *his* Dapple, portrayed by Parisian painter Paul Delaroche (1797-1859). There is the warrior, staring at the artist, with no earmuffs or gloves, riding on a beleaguered donkey up an icy slope among other soldiers and struggling animals. How different a perspective, and one that actually documents Napoleon's crossing of the Alps in the year 1800 on mule-back, from the earlier version of the scene, painted by Jacques-Louis David (1748–1825) entitled "The First Consul crossing the Alps at the Grand-Saint-Bernard Pass." Charles IV of Spain commissioned the work, in which the suffering donkey/mule has been upstaged by a rearing

OPPOSITE: BONAPARTE CROSSING THE ALPS, 1848. PAUL DELAROCHE

stallion. It was one of four versions of the same Romantic propaganda that David and his studio interns churned out. The artist determined the donkey too lowly a creature for purposes of empire building and manifest destiny. Hannibal would not have crossed these same glacial monsters on a donkey, or so said David. Ironic, since by the late Middle Ages in the early twelfth century, the popularity of pictorial and sculptural depictions of the donkey carrying the Holy Family on their flight to Egypt, illustrating a passage from Matthew 2:14, had hardly begun to peak.

That same donkey emerges in one of its earliest incarnations in the remarkable late fouteenth-century Dijon Altarpiece at the Musee des Beaux-Arts in the Burgundian capital of Dijon. This double-winged tempera work on wood, executed by the Duke of Burgundy, Philip the Bold's Netherlandish court painter, Melchior Broederlam (1381-1409), interprets the scene from Matthew with a donkey clearly represented as the source of deliverance. This is paradise in three-dimensional splendor. If we are to take literally the journey described in the masterpiece, it is the donkey that is closest to achieving its destination. His head reaches to the far right of the panel. The surrounding wilderness, all of the ecological clues within the painting that suggest a rugged journey, the flowers, the rocky peaks, the magnificent golden sky and the flying bird, combine to give the donkey a stature like no other being. Ahead in his humility, if you will.

This preeminence is accorded the donkey in the three solemn and joyful paintings by the Italian masters Gentile Da Fabriano (1370?-1427) in *The Magi's Adoration*; Domenico Ghirlandaio (1449-1494) in *Adoration of the Shepherds*; and Jacopo Bassano (1515-1592)

in his own version of *Adoration of the Shepherds*. Quentin Metsys
(1466–1530) lent absolute religious fervor to the relationship of a
mothering donkey with the Christ child by placing the smiling, be-
nevolent donkey closest compositionally of all creatures on earth
to Him, closer than Mary, Joseph or the angels.

REST ON THE FLIGHT INTO EGYPT (DETAIL FROM THE ALTARPIECE
OF THE PASSION). MELCHOIR BROEDERLAM, 1393–1399

Michelangelo Merisi da Caravaggio (1571–1610) lends another
twist to the donkey in his growing importance, figuratively and
metaphorically, by representing him in the role of either voyeur or
muse to an angel who performs a lullaby in his own *Rest on Flight
to Egypt* (1695–97). There is Joseph holding the pages of music,
with a sizeable, all-curious donkey standing behind and between

ADORATION OF THE SHEPHERDS. DOMENICO GHIRLANDAIO, CA. 1485

*REST ON
THE FLIGHT
INTO EGYPT.
CARAVAGGIO.
1596–97*

THE FLIGHT INTO EGYPT. GEORGES TRUBERT, CA. 1469

Joseph and the angel. Caravaggio, with the glint in his donkey's fantastic eye, suggests a potential ambiguity in the relationship of Mary and Joseph.[14] Suggestive and subjective, it is certainly a unique take on what was a fairly standard artistic interpretation of Biblical text.

The donkey is omnipresent in many of the great French manuscript illuminations of the late fifteenth century, Georges Trubert's, among others; as well as in the famed *Book of Hours* tradition, a kind of *Farmer's Almanac* of the Renaissance or prayer book devoted to the rhythms of nature as they entered into peoples' lives.

From I Fu-chiu's *Sage on a Donkey*, a hanging scroll painted in Japan in the 1720s, to the wonderful sepia photographs of donkeys by Charles F. Lummis (1859-1928), to Marc Chagall's *Blue Donkey* (1887-1985)—this uniquely appealing creature has become a spiritual centerpiece.

Nineteenth century British painters John Crome and Thomas Sidney Cooper were especially attracted to the rural setting for animals. Cooper (1803-1902) would be remembered as "Cow Cooper" for his remarkable ability to elicit the gentle demeanor and

BLUE DONKEY, MARC CHAGALL, 1925

FOUR BURROS. THOMAS SIDNEY COOPER, CA. 1830

dignity of so-called farm animals. He could as easily be thought of as "Donkey Cooper" given his numerous paintings of wandering families of donkeys among sheep, executed during his most prolific decade, 1846–1856. These are unforgettable paintings, as are those of the Belgian painter, Eugene Joseph Verboeckhoven (1798–1881), who had so influenced Cooper during his period in Brussels in the late 1820s. While Queen Victoria had commissioned him to paint the royal herd of Jersey cows, Cooper's insistence on presenting to the world the real donkey is what best captures his genius for depicting empathy. Crome similarly captured, in the 1820s, the enchanted semi-wild, semi-domesticated ethos of Norwich, much in the manner of his contemporary, John Constable and scores of earlier seventeenth century Dutch masters. Crome's small and modest equines melt into the landscape, abiding there with an aesthetic conviction that resonates to this day. During that time, however, most English rural folk depended on their donkeys for trans-

"It Tastes Good to Me"

port, just as horses were the harnessed engines of the British urban economy. And the earliest attempts to achieve legislation that might soften the burden upon equines in Parliament from 1800 to 1822 were typically mocked by those who used the "ass" as a symbol of the folly inherent to all animal rights considerations.

Nonetheless, the bond between equines and humanity continued to evolve. Consider the photographic opportunities afforded the human-donkey relationship long explored by photographers who clearly found the animals captivating and adorable. Two works, in particular, stand out: *Burros: A Collection of Sixty-Four Cute, Curious and Interesting Burro Pictures* by H. H. Tammen (Denver, Colorado: The H. H. Tammen Curio Co., 1902) and *The Burro Book* by S. M. McCandless (Pueblo, Colorado: S. M. McCandless Publisher, 1900). The latter assemblage of text and imagery is especially interesting in terms of its introduction, which argues that the burro is a native of Spain; is basically responsible for the creation of Western Civilization with its trains, towns, railroads and mines; can eat essentially anything, or nothing; and is—for all of his industry—essentially "opposed to progress." Curiously, this amazing creature is said to be tougher than the mule,

{94}

an assertion usually reversed by most writers when describing donkeys, burros, wild asses and mules. But what is truly wonderful about the prefatory remarks McCandless writes of the donkey is the following: "His philosophy is beautiful. . . . The children all love him. The little Indian plays round his heels without concern, the tiny Mexican wreathes his neck with yucca bloom, while the eastern child visitor proudly mounts upon his back and belabors him into a gentle walk. . . . The mountaineer's baby shares his meal with bay burro, and they sleep together under the pines. His patient, cheerful, little figure has become so strongly identified with the west and southwest that the portraits here given cannot fail to awaken some pleasant thought in the minds of those who look upon them."[15]

And what are the subjects of the portraits? Many of their titles say it all for better or worse: "Playmates," "A Band of Brothers," "I Helped To Build The Pike's Peak Railroad," "Chrysanthemum,"

"CHRYSANTHEMUM"

"Lumber For The Mine," "Weary Pilgrim," "A Sentimental Journey," "Mamma's Baby," "Rags, That's Me," "Burro Alley, Santa
Fe," "Baby's First Walk," "A Mountain Excursion," "Diego And
His Donkey, Pueblo De Taos," "Mexican Beggars," "Chief Frances-
co," "Reflections," "A Happy Family," "Here's Your Share, Snow-
ball," "Burros Loaded With Straw, Mexico," "Take Me Back Home
To Mother," and lastly, "The Pioneer's Friend."

Many of the same photographs appear in McCandless and Tammen, although often with different titles. In Tammen, there is also
an introduction which includes the following: ". . . all people love
the burro...Oh, the little dear! Mama, buy me one! . . . And so the
burro is a constant joy. . . . He will do anything that he can and will

OSAGE WOMAN AT AN ARKANSAS OZARK RESORT, CA. 1940

attempt things that he can not do, if only he is urged...nobody can be really angry with him. The miner, the hunter, the mountaineer, the Indian, all depend on him, and everybody in the West has a tender spot for the friendly little beast....Various traits of character are evinced to one who studies the burro. There are jaunty burros, melancholy burros, high-headed burros, proud and independent burros, and burros possessing many other interesting traits. ..."[16]

These burros would be painted, etched and sculpted by numerous southwestern artists such as Joseph Bakos, Randall Davies, Charles Russell, Willard Clark and the Chicago-based Emil Armin. Armin's brilliant red etching, *Mountain Farm, Santa Fe*, 1928, is the same sturdy animal, one may surmise, that Darwin referred to in Uruguay on his 1845 voyage on the Beagle, when he wrote of the miraculous powers of the mule contending that "art has here outdone nature."[17]

ADOBE MAKERS. JOZEF G. BAKOS, 1928

Think of the aforementioned caption, ". . . he will do anything he can and will attempt things that he can not do, if only he is urged. . . ." From a poetic point of view, the donkey is inspired, like a flying fish, or the great artist willing to hang upside down for three years to paint the Sistine Chapel. Donkeys are unpredictable and accomplish things of which we are unaware. It is the same throughout the animal world, from Zebra Finches learning new music from their tutors, to a dog that kept running back into the collapsing World Trade Center to rescue person after person. What do we really know about animals? What can we say with accuracy about ourselves? When the great eternal questions about life plague us with self-doubt and uncertainty, animals can still invoke magnificent mystery and constant surprise.

These few above-mentioned references scarcely touch the vast realm of donkey-related art, photography, and literature. A history of landscape art is yet to be written around the subject donkey, but he is central in every era, in every format and style, from the pastoral and Arcadian traditions, to the photographic obsessions of the nineteenth and early twentieth centuries. The donkey looms in our creative work as a divining rod of society's relationship to the natural world; an intermediary, if you will, that facilitated our approach to God, to the wilderness, to ethics in general and to the development of civilization.

The donkey mirrors—as did Dapple for Cervantes—the human condition. These very donkeys coming towards us this moment are the offspring of the whole history of donkeys, beginning in the blurred distance of some desert horizon of Algeria, Nubia and the Eastern Sudan, of some Tibetan outback on the edges of the Himalayas where the equally charismatic Bactrian camel and

WHITE MAN'S BURDEN.
CHARLES M. RUSSELL

MOUNTAIN FARM, SANTA FE. EMILE ARMIN, 1928

Asian wild ass (dziggetai in Mongolian or *Equus hemionus*) listened
to the music of herders gathered together each night. They come
from the domestic African races, possibly Egyptian, brilliantly
white, durable, glowing, a soft edge; and from Rome, and Ethiopia,
Somalia and France. They come from the wild snowy Pyrenees,
the rainy forests of Normandy and the windy, warm Mediterranean climes of Provence. In France, they correspond in their geographic distribution to the Cistercian monasteries of the Middle
Ages that were renowned for their "architecture of silence."[18] These
were monasteries founded on the rule of seventh century St. Bene-

FROM *ANIMATED NATURE*. WILLIAM DANIELL, 1809

dict who created an Order of working monks who farmed, strolled through haunted forests of the Morvan and collaborated in the pursuit of their spiritual path with donkeys, themselves monastic denizens on an equally spiritual journey.

In Jain traditions from ancient India, every individual is divine, endowed with a soul, or *jiva*, that must be allowed to evolve in its own way, on its own path. Jains are vegetarian with no known custom of keeping donkeys (or any animal). But Jains have created *panjorapors*, animal sanctuaries throughout the Indian sub-continent. In such refuges, equines have been given protection and accorded all the respect a guru would receive. In Medieval France, while donkeys were clearly used for labor, the Benedictines must have held a special place in their hearts for donkeys, whose images can today be read in the revolutionary genre of sacred manuscript illumination beginning in the twelfth century where life forms—man, donkey, birds, plants—all communed in the glory of God. Perhaps

the greatest expression of this religious and aesthetic jubilation can be seen in the exquisite *Book of Hours by the Master of Mary of Burgundy*, also known as *The Hours of Engelbert of Nassau*, executed sometime between 1470 and 1490.[19]

It thrills us to remember how critical these gorgeous beings are to our own human history and cultural core, and it gives us great joy to be able to reflect on these poetic reveries that donkeys have elicited in the imagination of our own species.

ST. FRANCIS IN THE DESERT. GIOVANNI BELLINI, CA. 1480

The Quiet Solace
of Donkeys

*D*onkeyphilia, the love of donkeys, is our own word, inspired by and in homage to the splendid word coined in 1984 by Harvard biologist, Edward O. Wilson: "biophilia."[1] Biophilia, simply defined, is the love among species, the sympathy that life forms share with fellow creatures.

We believe that most donkeys, if given the chance, would fashion a world without violence. Like St. Francis of Assisi, they would re-make the natural world into a proverbial Garden of Eden, wherein the lion and the lamb lay side by side as described in the Book of Isaiah, the image conveyed by so many paradise painters, from Jan Brueghel the Elder (who painted a series of sketches of donkeys in 1615)[2] to Edward Hicks, whose *Peaceable Kingdom* may be well-known to contemporary readers. It is no surprise then that certain people would have a natural affinity with donkeys. Leo Tolstoy's philosophy of non-violence, which would hugely influence Mahatma Gandhi, was shared by his eldest daughter Tatiana Sukhotin-Tolstoy. Tatiana, at the age of thirteen, noted in her diary on the 11th of November, 1878, "We have two donkeys, we ride them every day. Outwards they walk but homewards ... if you let them, they're off at the gallop. One is called Bismarck, the other MacMahon...."[3] We wonder how much the innocence, vulnerability and gentleness of those two donkeys may have affected Tolstoy, the peace-loving giant of world literature.

Nearly four hundred years earlier, Leonardo da Vinci left his own insight into the equine world unfinished but intimated in a note from April 23, 1490, writing that he had "resumed work on the horse," a clay model for a commission by the ruler of Milan,

Ludovico Sforza. This was to be a horse that would have become one of the greatest wonders of the world, measuring some twenty-four feet of gleaming bronze from its withers to the earth, bigger than Michelangelo's *David*.[4] Leonardo's voracious lust for depicting the natural world occasionally embraced a donkey: first, in a drawing of a donkey and a bull,[5] as peaceful an image as Leonardo's human portraits; and then, amid the welter of other equines who lounge in the resort-like palace seen as part of his *Study for the Background of the 'Adoration of the Magi' in the Uffizi Gallery of Florence* in 1481.

The *donkeyphilia* paradigm comports with others that are aesthetically driven by the myth, if not the reality, of pastoralism. Consider the two-humped Bactrian camels of the Gobi desert, critically endangered with fewer than a thousand remaining, whose love of music and willingness to adopt orphans and suckle them was demonstrated gorgeously in the movie *The Story of the Weeping Camel*.[6] Gazelles in the Sahara have been shown to also embrace other species and raise them among themselves. Jean-Claude Armen, an anthropologist, wrote of a wild child raised by such gazelles in a remarkable story with all the trappings of a myth seemingly too good to be true.[7] And, for every such tale as Carlo Collodi's *Story Of A Puppet, Or The Adventures Of Pinocchio*—as it was originally titled when published in 1883[8]—in which the donkey's form spells torment for the child, a wealth of other literature, for children of all ages celebrates donkeys and underscores community, interdependency, and loving kindness throughout the animal world.

You can see this among the donkeys' close relatives. Zebras graze contentedly in parts of East Africa alongside dozens of other species from egrets and Cape Buffalo to hippos, elephants, gazelles and antelopes. And, they drink at watering holes alongside lions, cheetahs and leopards. French shepherds have long known that donkeys will defend a flock of sheep with their lives; that the milk of a jenny or jennet has less fat content and more sugar than a cow's milk and this is thought to give the female donkey her incredibly sweet demeanor—ideal as a companion for children. Moreover, that same milk was alleged to have given Cleopatra her fine skin (her beauty baths rumored to have used the milk of "two hundred lactating jennies").[9] Poppea, the wife of the emperor Nero, is also said to have bathed in donkey milk. Donkeys have, by their meditative manner, instilled a reverence in all those who come into contact with them, from soldiers to shepherds to children to those who rely upon donkeys to assist them in physical therapy.

DONKEYPHILIA SÉANCE

In speaking of biophilia, E. O. Wilson says that human beings are human, in part, because of how they relate to other organisms. That is his general conclusion. But, in considering the particulars of humans' varying treatment and maltreatment of animals, the donkey seems to reside in the middle somewhere. He/she may be a pet or a wild creature. The truly wild donkeys are as rare, or rarer, than African wild dogs. Some donkeys have been eaten, many tormented and many adored, having experienced enough of human behavior to be wary of, or to love us.

Donkeys are among the most eloquent diplomats in the natural world. So are songbirds, whales and dolphins, lions and loons, wolves, coyotes, lyrebirds and morning doves. But, it has been in the company of donkeys that we have had the opportunity to picnic in woods and meadows. Those picnics are the essence of a *donkeyphilia* séance, and they evoke every possible reverie of the proverbial pastoralist tradition with shepherds musing on their staffs, daydreaming about their lost or absent love amid their grazing sheep and donkeys.

Pastoral to perfection, Batman and Robin roamed the forests and fields together, aloof from the other herds. When the weather was inclement, they wandered into barn stalls and made them-

OLD FRIENDS

selves at home. They were long-time companions who preferred each other's company to that of their neighbors. And, they kept their distance from us. Maybe that is why we were so drawn to them.

When Batman revealed his age and need of a special diet, he and his best friend, Robin, were moved together to a milder coastal environment for care. Eventually, Robin lost an ailing Batman. On our last visit, Robin approached Jane for the first time ever and buried her head in Jane's breast sharing her sorrow over Batman. Robin wouldn't let Jane leave her side. Robin has yet to pal up with another of her kind. She is presently keeping company with a stallion named Galahad.

Some have argued that domestication is a co-evolutionary phenomenon (the opportunistic distribution theory), that some animals may have even domesticated *us* with mutually beneficial results. Stephen Budiansky[10] goes so far as to suggest that certain farm animals used humans for their own benefit. As described by Laurie Winn Carlson,[11] "domesticated plants and animals were really interlopers seeking an opportunity for easier survival." This is, indeed, a curious theory. If it holds up, it suggests an even greater responsibility on the part of humans to take care of the animals who have placed their trust in us. There seems to be something to the notion that donkeys have relished their connection to other creatures that show them respect and love.

The picnic is about love, to be sure. And not just love of a cookie. And somehow we feel it is the fitting description of that intriguing conviviality wherein there is shared laughter, the passing around of food, the goosing, gumption, frivolous delight. We delight in an outdoor repast with our donkey friends—their eyes are bright, heads bobbing, a bit of cavorting, dodging, grooming, tender mooning and other activities indicating a positively wonderful immersion in the fields of heaven.

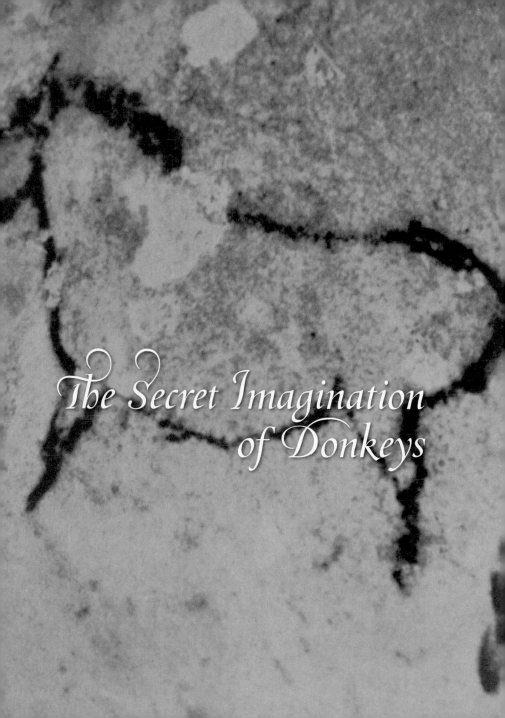

The Secret Imagination of Donkeys

HORSE IN NORMANDY

OVERLEAF: ROUFFIGNAC CAVE IN THE DORDOGNE, FRANCE

*f*or early Paleolithic peoples, equine images figured with as much prominence as did the earliest bird depictions. Mayan and Aztec animal cults were more likely to feature the jaguar as well as birds, and ancient Egyptian representations largely focused upon such gods and goddesses as Hathor, the cow goddess; Apis, the bull god; the cobra; the hippopotamus; the vulture; the crocodile and the monkey. Western and Asiatic animal repertoire largely featured equines and birds.

Two of countless French rocky inner sanctums from twenty to thirty thousand years ago, Bedeilhac Cave in the region of Tarascon-sur-Ariege, and Lascaux Cave in the Dordogne, are distinguished by their gorgeous equine portraits. The figures have been described as steppe horses and ponies, but they could easily be called donkeys. There is no way to physiologically or aesthetically distinguish them. They are magical, mysterious and gentle, intimating the wandering imagination with which they were clearly and deliberately evoked.

These early depictions collectively suggest a mystique that was deeply felt by our predecessors when they first took to painting. Reindeer, bulls, equines—these were the animals that took priority over all others, even man. The animal paintings span a suite of species, from ibex and heron to woolly mammoth, but it is an equine, most perfectly captured at the center of what is called "The Grand Plafond" of the Rouffignac Cave in the Dordogne, that stands out as the source of perennial meditation. We see the same equine in motion in the Santimamine Cave in Vizcaya, Spain.

Near Palermo, Sicily, at a cavern called Addaura on Monte Pellegrino, both humans and equines appear together. Two animals side by side are listening to something the humans are saying. Their ears are up and it is clear that they are donkeys.[1]

The ancient attempt to understand nature was more a series of divinations through art and folklore than any systematic effort that, today, we would describe as scientific. Yet, despite that "imagination in which scraps of folk-lore, travelers' tales and fragments of misapprehended science"[2] were assembled into the first collections of marvels, wonders, chronicles and colloquies—the earliest studies drawn from nature were, in fact, marvelous and wonderful. Commentators may have suffered confusion in their varied compilations, juxtaposing the "mystical, magical and moral" as ornithologist/historian James Fisher has pointed out.[3] The *Physiologos*, one of the earliest works of natural history, completed either in Egypt or Syria by 370 AD, and covering a vast range of subjects from nature, was—for all of the splendid faults Fisher indicates—the precursor of the next 1,200 years of studies, be they allegorical, fabulist, or Platonic.[4]

Consider how the donkey fared over that vast timeframe, starting with the provocative amusements told in the wake of Greek and Roman animism, insightful stories which made their own suitable claims to the human sources in nature through poetry, humor, illustration and adventure tales.

Long after losing his golden touch, King Midas was said to have been present for a musical competition between Pan and Apollo. When the God Tmolus declared Apollo's lyre more melodious than Pan's pipe, Midas disagreed, favoring Pan. Apollo is said to have instantly changed the King's ears into those of a donkey. Midas, appalled and ashamed, covered himself with a purple turban and demanded that all those in his court never disclose the truth. However, his barber whispered the fact that the King had donkey ears into a hole in a field. The grasses that grew over that hole betrayed the secret to a gentle southern wind a year later. Then, all the world was to learn of his transformation.[5]

The donkey as subject of a literary work of art made his real debut in the epic by Apuleius Apuleius (born 124 AD), titled *Asinus Aureus*, and known in English as *Metamorphoses* or *The Golden Ass*. It is considered to be the only novel in the Latin of Roman times that has survived entire. And its glory is the fact that its world-roving protagonist, Lucius (the semi-autobiographic Apuleius himself) becomes a donkey, and spends much of the story experiencing every possible turmoil and vain hope of which donkeys are capable, at least when speaking Latin.[6]

The whole epic, beginning in Thessaly (where legend has it the Centaurs—creatures half man, half horse—originated) pivots upon Lucius' comedic revelations while spying upon a woman, Pamphile, who transforms herself with the aid of a certain potion, into an owl. Lucius himself attempts it, only to choose the wrong

vial which, with equally astounding witchcraft, turns him into a splendid ass.

That is only the beginning. His donkey persona is deemed valuable by thieves, and then by the most beautiful maiden in the world who promises him literary glory if he will let her ride him away from her captors. The escape fails, although the maiden is eventually liberated. But for Lucius, unrelenting bad luck is his only compass as he finds himself next condemned to the rough mating rituals of a large stud, more than once. Then he is demonized by a sadistic little monster. No matter how meritorious his intentions are, Lucius is overtaken by woe upon woe. As all of Roman history is collapsing around him with killings, suicides, crucifixions, marauding wolves, carnivorous ants, Lucius—in the form of an ass—finds himself about to be slaughtered on the butcher's block, then variously tormented by a baker's wife, dispatched to the care of a gardener, and to cooks. Finally, a magician recognizes Lucius' intelligence and devises a money-making scheme that would see a lusty woman having sex with him in public. This bestiality is accompanied by more twists that worsen by the moment until, finally, praying in the moonlight, Lucius is saved by a goddess, Isis, who restores him to his human physique after which he is ultimately reunited with his horse and his family.

The Golden Ass as well as the story of King Midas are not unlike *A Midsummer Night's Dream.* In Shakespeare's madcap play, the sparring and jealous king of the fairies, Oberon, sets his servant Puck to punish his queen, by first turning Nick Bottom the Weaver into a donkey-headed man, and then applying a potion to the sleeping Titania's eyes so she will fall madly in love with the

first creature she sees upon waking. This happens to be the hapless Nick who, when he wakes begins to sing (bray). His song awakens the Queen who is instantly smitten and has her fairy servants attend him. When the antidote is applied Titania tells Oberon of her strange dream. Nick is sadly returned to human form, and the play has an otherwise happy ending. The wild adventure told by the satirical Platonic philosopher and literary genius Lucius Apuleius, of a feckless Roman wayfarer in the form of *Equus asinus*, set the stage for all future picaresque literary works of the Renaissance: Alain-Rene Lesage's *Gil Blas*, Hans Von Grimmelhausen's *The Adventures of Simplicius Simplicissimus*, the works of Rabelais, Boccaccio and Cervantes. In the eighteenth and nineteenth and twentieth centuries, there were scores of books featuring donkeys as cameo or central presences. These yarns bore such titles as *The Adventures Of A Donkey*, by Arabella Argus, London, 1815.[7] In fact, nearly two thousand years later, another epic told through the eyes of a donkey, would elaborate upon the suffering undergone by the Golden Ass: the film director Robert Bresson's *Au Hasard, Balthazar* (1966). Balthazar is a donkey first introduced as a foal beloved by a young girl, who then undergoes countless vagaries at the hands of a series of owners; sad twists, and deeply melancholic experiences. One critic writes, "The donkey Balthazar, is one of the most intriguing and powerful in all cinema...where Balthazar is on his own (or in the company of other animals) are some of the most extraordinary cinematic scenes ever imagined, let alone realized."[8] Two scenes are particularly compelling: at a circus Balthazar

OVERLEAF: *Scene from a Midsummer Night's Dream, Titania and Bottom*. Edwin Landseer, 1848–1861

walks past a tiger's cage and the two animals stare at one another. A captive polar bear also gazes yearningly at the donkey. And at the end of a tortured life, abandoned by the self-absorbed, indifferent people who populate the film, Balthazar—with contraband hanging from his back—and blood oozing from a gunshot wound, lies down in the mountains amid a flock of sheep who witness his death. It is a cruel, unflinching portrait of an innocent who endures torment and longs for lost love.

In 2002, Russian director Timur Kurbanaliev made a twenty-six minute film entitled "About Donkeys"[9] which promotes yet a different set of characteristics which have by now become quite legendary, namely, the donkey's mysterious nature and continually "unexpected behavior."

But Lucius's story is the ultimate metaphor for what the donkey would mean to humanity. He is also a true character, in and

THE FABLES OF AESOP, PARAPHRAS'D IN VERSE, BY JOHN OGILBY, 1668

out of fiction. His didactic lessons for the rest of us were presaged in the equally fantastic life of the strange, intangible character whose name posterity would remember as Aesop, a seventh century BC author whose legendary *Fables* were more than likely tales from the oral storytelling tradition, collected posthumously by Babrius and then by Phaedrus. They were eventually published in the fourteenth century by the monk Maximus Planudes. Aesop's ass was magnificently illustrated by the Bohemian artist, Wenceslaus Hollar (1607–1677) and his circle of colleagues. Hollar was among the finest of stylists when it came to etching that back-country, populated by equines of every hybrid, with paradise

NOAH'S ARK;
BEFORE THE DELUGE.
HANS BOL, LATE 16TH
CENTURY, ENGRAVED BY
GERARD DE JODE

evocations to all sides. Hollar's animal etchings equate beautifully with Aesop's own interpretations, particularly with regard to the repeated tales told of the ass's exquisitely refined humility, a steadfast voice of reason amid a welter of human folly compounded by the chaos unleashed by humanity against all other animal species. The "animals" get their revenge, of course, and these are the messages of which Aesop warned us: our cruelty and stupidity would

ET ANIMALIA VTRIVSQVE SEXVS. GEN.: VI.

inevitably backfire. The ass knows more than others, and his rear-end kick seems to be a gesture driven by the frustration that history keeps repeating itself.[10]

We see the donkey's profound imaginative dilemma in the very first two volumes of the twelve-volume *The Book of the Thousand Nights and a Night*.[11] Almost from the beginning, "The Third Shaykh's Story" opens with the passage, "Know, O Sultan and

POST ANNVM, NOE CVM OMNIB: EGREDITVR.

head of the Jann, that this mule was my wife."[12] The second volume describes how the ass was the last animal to enter Noah's Ark, and brought with it the Iblis, or devil, such is the low regard accorded this animal whose profound altruism, his hesitancy to save even himself was misinterpreted by Noah, who then inadvertently brought evil into the world.[13] Christian tradition contests this Islamic version of the donkey's relationship to the ark. Dutch mas-

FERT HOLOCAVSTA DOMINO GEN VIII

ter Hans Bol (1534-93) did two scenes of Noah's Ark, one before and one after the Deluge. As engraved by the Flemish artist Gerard de Jode (1509-1591) two donkeys, male and female, are among the very first to enter the ark. The scene suggests that we are only seeing part of the mad migration into the waiting ark, and others are yet to arrive. After the deluge, the donkeys appear to be among the last to leave the Ark.[14]

Furthering the logic that donkeys are intrinsic to the Creation is a mosaic from the third century AD, in Sicily, in which the god Orpheus sits beneath the tree of life playing his lyre for all the animals. The top-most creatures depicted are birds and a donkey, one that appears to be a zebra hybrid.[15] The donkey's ears are fully attuned to the music. It was this same wild stellar beast that would be transformed from the statuesque horse of Greek coinage and the likenesses in marble from the Parthenon into that other hybrid, said to be synonymous with Christ, the most beautiful and threatened of all creatures, namely, the self-sacrificing unicorn, who is the subject of more speculation and mystery than any other Renaissance being. Heavenly love, religious closure, the Virgin and the Garden of Eden were all incarnate in its magical demeanor. Its countenance is all-knowing. This unicorn, as seen in the tapestry at the Cluny Museum in Paris, we perceive as the glorified donkey, with all the complex traits with which humans have endowed him over time. Persian tradition even speaks of a three-legged ass with six eyes and a golden-colored horn living in the middle of the ocean. So pure is he/she, its manure consists of amber. Jorge Luis Borges refers to this wonderful imaginary donkey as having first been observed and detailed by Zarathustra. Later, the creature was mentioned in a book entitled *Bundahish*.[16]

Yet, the perfect donkey/unicorn is imperiled, as witnessed in its depiction in the late Flemish or French tapestry from the Chateau of Verteuil, a gift by John D. Rockefeller Jr., in 1937, to the Cloisters Collection of the Metropolitan Museum of Art in New York. There, the unicorn is savagely killed by hunters. The *Koran* refers to the braying of an ass as coming from hell. But one could ascribe an alternative explanation for this: the donkey's plaintive cry mirrors the horrors it has endured in all of its incarnations, both wild and domestic. It is stridently, unambiguously warning humanity of humans' own bestiality. Perhaps it was this very ambivalence that prompted Jules Renard, in his tormented *Histoires Naturelles*, to describe the donkey's cry as one that brays "to extinction."[17]

All such attributions of character invested in donkeys are matters of imagination. They give us to understand that what we see in a donkey, the donkey sees in us. That whatever emotions are elicited in their presence, they are experiencing reciprocally. If this is true, and we believe it to be so, then the world is entirely different than "civilization" would have us think. In fact, we must start over and lay aside all differences, all species prejudice or egocentrism. We must make peace and give in to the very joy the child in each of us would engender. This inspired and inspiring aspect of the donkey was brought out most lovingly by the Reverend W. Bingley in his 1805 *Animal Biography*.[18] Bingley writes of an old man who, for many years sold vegetables in London and with the assistance of his donkey moved from household to household. People noticed how the vegetable vender loved his donkey. He never once used a stick to goad him, or harm him in any way and they asked "whether his beast was not apt to be stubborn" to which the old man replied that "he is ready to do anything, or go anywhere. I bred him myself. He is sometimes playful and skittish; and once ran away from me; and while more than fifty people were after him, laughing and trying to stop him, he suddenly turned back of himself, and never stopped till he ran his head kindly into my bosom."

TRAVELS WITH A DONKEY IN THE CÉVENNES, 1879.
ROBERT LOUIS STEVENSON, ILLUSTRATED BY WALTER CRANE

In similar fashion, Robert Louis Stevenson realizes how much he loves his donkey, but only after selling him for all of twenty-five francs at the end of a long journey through France. He proclaims, "...I became aware of my bereavement. I had lost Modestine. Up to that moment I had thought I hated her; but now she was gone, 'And, O, The difference to me!' . . . She loved to eat out of my hand. She was patient, elegant in form . . . her virtues were her own. . . . Father Adam wept when he sold her to me; after I had sold her in my turn, I was tempted to follow his example; and being alone . . . I did not hesitate to yield to my emotion." That is how Stevenson concludes the entire book, at the end of his twelve day journey with Modestine.[19]

How shall we account for Stevenson's twelve days of oblivion? Is this what it takes for a sophisticated, world-weary artist to recognize divinity in nature: to realize that a donkey has meant everything to him? In a curious little book from the mid-nineteenth century, an anonymous writer refers to the ass as "the most despised and the worst-used of all animals, and yet the one on which the greatest honour has been put . . ."[20] referring to the fact that Christ went humbly on the donkey's back into Jerusalem from the Mount of Olives trailed by all those poor followers. "Behold, your king is coming to you; He is just and endowed with salvation, Humble, and mounted on a donkey . . ." Zechariah 9:9–10. The author commends passages from Numbers (CHAPTER XXII) and Exodus (XXIII) in which we are called upon to show mercy to one another and to all animals, with the focus concentrated on that ass, as well as upon the ox. When Cesare Ripa wrote his *Iconologia* in Rome in 1593—with its nearly two hundred animal symbols—he

ASINUS (ESEL) *HISTORIAE NATURALIS DE AUIBUS LIBRI 6.*
JOHANN JONSTON, 1650

was artistically bringing together one of the earliest poetic field studies that insisted on the equal playing field between humans and other species. And, Leo Baptista Alberti wrote his treatise on equine mechanics and physiology, *De equo animante* (ca. 1438), for purposes of proposing perfect, indeed divine, proportions that might serve as a model for all anatomy and, by inference, behavior.

One sees a similar indebtedness to imaginative equines in the illustrations to a 1721 edition of Chaucer's collected works, figuring the most elegant of horses and animals that seem transitional between horse and mule, spiritual, fluid in their canter, as animated as the most spirited donkey.[21] By the mid-seventeen hun-

dreds, Jean-Baptiste Oudry would draw 276 animals, taken from life, to illustrate the *Fables* of Jean de La Fontaine written beginning in 1668. And, in the famed two-volume animal *Fables* of John Gay, and the remarkable five-volume illustrated *Orlando Furioso* by Lodovico Ariosto, translated by John Hoole in London in 1785, dozens of spectacular equines lend celestial credibility to the fact that this family of mammals has no peer. Many of the greatest illustrators—from Leonardo da Vinci (1452-1519) to two other great Italians, Andrea del Verrocchio (1435-88) and Ulysse Aldrovandi, who painted *Alces alces*, a delicate, gently smiling donkey with antlers[22]—have seen in the equine the ultimate preference in nature, a being whose divine proportions mirrored a moral core that could

THE ENTRY INTO JERUSALEM, SIMON BENING

serve as an exemplar for our own kind. It was almost as if every element in the world had come together by way of some parliamentary confessional wherein the equine translated to best in show.

Donkeys and their immediate relatives, whether horse or zebra, have always been favored by both spiritual and political thinkers. Coleridge, who literary scholar David Perkins has described, was smitten with a donkey in the fall of 1794. The animal was encountered grazing on the lawns of Jesus College, and the bond that the poet would form with him, as he had with a mythic albatross, would become the basis for his important poem, "To a Young Ass." [23] Coleridge would refer to the animal as his "Brother," an attribution that led many to assume he was not only referencing his adamant belief that no cruelty to animals should ever be

tolerated, but to a Utopian England that would harmoniously balance differences between the poor and the rich, abolishing slavery,
and throwing in for good measure a Revolution in France with its
famed mottos proclaiming liberty.

Not surprisingly, the range of attributions involving equines is
enormous because horses and donkeys were utilized for warfare,
including the carrying of military or expeditionary equipment,
while simultaneously figuring in so much religious representation,
from Roelandt Savery's (1576–1639) animal paradise paintings

to Pablo Picasso's *Guernica*. In a panel from the Church of Santo Domenico in Bologna, for example, a horse is actually portrayed kneeling devotionally. And, in a tiny painting by Domenico Beccafumi (ca.1486–1551) which hangs in the Louvre, there is Saint Anthony standing bowed in a courtyard holding a wooden bowl containing the Host, as a donkey kneels before him. It is called *St. Anthony and the Miracle of the Mule*. It is but one of many artistic representations of the legend.

The history of art and letters, of eco science and biology, for all of their revelatory power, fall short before the truth of donkeys themselves; that is obviously so with every variety and every individual. The donkeys we know have entered our lives by way of any number of deep recesses in the psyche and subconscious, gaps which science cannot fill. Their history in art, literature and religion singles them out as gifted, targeted and tenacious. Eco-psychologists might well think of them as some kind of balm for self-healing, and they wouldn't be wrong. Historians certainly adduce much of the sociology of labor by incorporating donkeys into the formula. Comparative anatomy suggests that their missing lumbar vertebra is the explanation for their greater stamina out on the trail, trundling loads. And, some sanctuaries think of them as the ideal candidates for petting zoos because of their perceived tenderness and dependability.

All these assumptions and assertions are true and untrue. Donkeys may well be important to human stability, but only for those who have the luck or wisdom to spend time in their company, and who have learned to maintain a respectful distance when instructed by the donkeys themselves to do so. Donkeys give clear signals

of warning when they want not to be tangled with. So, it is critical
to remain conscious and respectful when in their presence.

Four themes illuminate the different guises of the human perception of donkeys throughout time. First, Rembrandt painted
Rest on the Flight into Egypt in oils, but the donkey does not register.
However, five of his etchings do reveal the master's feelings about
donkeys. Two appear early in his career, in 1626. Both are "Rest
on the Flight into Egypt" scenes. Later he created a magnificent
Angel Appearing to the Shepherds in 1634. In 1651 and 1654, he detailed two other "Flight into Egypt" renditions. They are studies

MARK TWAIN'S PICTURE OF THE MATTERHORN, 1906

of sad, put-upon creatures. They suggest no salvation but only a sense of impending, painful doom. Similarly, his 1653 re-working of the artist Hercules Segers' *Flight into Egypt* reveals a donkey as solemn, dignified and unhappy as Mary, who sits barely awake on the murky animal, her legs dangling off his left side. Both Mary's head and that of the nameless donkey hang low.[24]

Now leap forward to a very different concept of a donkey burdened by our own restless dreams and nightmares: the East African explorers Burton and Speke, enormous, ungainly men astride two tiny donkeys on their quest for the source of the Nile. A newborn donkey is led on a leash between the two sparring men.[25] A third motif is conveyed by Mark Twain in his exquisite *A Tramp Abroad*. Leave it to the greatest wit in American history to conjure one of the greatest donkeys, ever. In chapter thirty-eight, in the midst of "scientific researches" atop the Gorner Grat summit, Twain provides a pivotal footnote and describes how he caught sight of the naked Matterhorn for just a moment, "leveled my photographic apparatus at it without the loss of an instant, and should have got an elegant picture if my donkey had not interfered...." And, there is Mark Twain's everlasting image of the Matterhorn with a massive plaything, a toy-like donkey of seemingly enormous proportions, standing on the glacier between the mountain and the artist, a donkey not about to be upstaged by a mere Matterhorn. It is comical, child-like and forever enshrines the wit's mindful, willful and conscious companion, the donkey.[26]

It is the same donkey, of sorts, painted by Harold Jones in an exquisite and obscure farm book he wrote and illustrated for children at the moment the world was plunged into the horrors of World War II. The book begins with the line, "One lovely summer's morning, Stephanie Angela awoke and sat up in her bed. She felt very happy...."[27] In her room are a doll, numerous books, a hobby-horse and donkeys, a cow and ducks on the table. It is a day to remember, the day her Mummie is taking her by train to visit their cousins John and Julia at White Gate Farm out in the country. Never has a farm been more splendidly appointed, with two donkeys grazing prominently side by side above the church spire, beneath the sunlit cloudy sky. A world of color and dreams with a windmill, children playing, cows freely wandering; a perfect world, in which these animals belong in no less way or measure than their human companions.

All of these images suggest a collective unconscious that seizes

upon donkeys with contradictions or conflicts that are ours alone. We can indulge flights of fancy, imagining donkeys to be gods of laughter or of forgiveness. But whatever we do, they will not suffer too much extraneous gibberish. Donkeys tolerate such intellectual tangents and footnotes only if they are covered in something delicious.

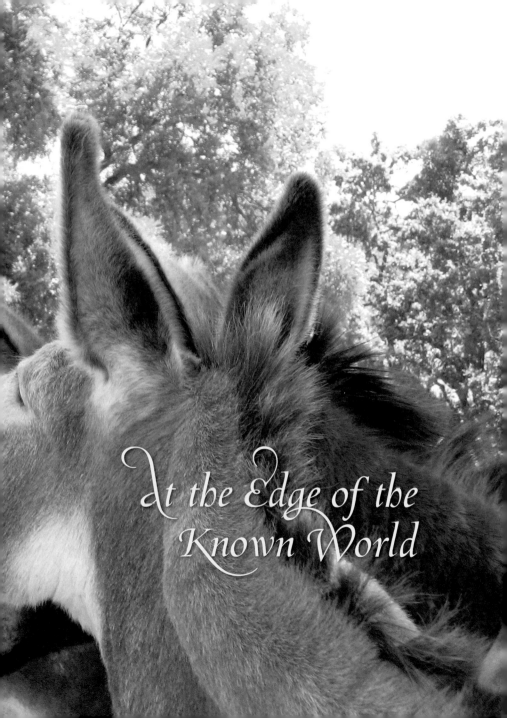

At the Edge of the
Known World

*I*t is raining. Sixty or so donkeys gather around us. It is one big happy family, no doubt about it: a brayer patch of jovial, squirming, feisty, cavorting life. Every one of us is angling to satisfy a desire. We are different and our differences seem to crave explication or investigation. Curiosity is as open and unstinting as a festival of babbling brooks.

The volitions are widely conveyed both physically and as an intermittent vociferous murmur of vocalizations. To what end?

We slow down the audio recordings and aurally behold a fascinating prospect. Something is going on which we had suspected though not recognized. There is an apparent dispatch of continuous donkey speech that hosts an endless variety of enunciations, subtleties and verb tenses. A few "frequency analyses" have been undertaken with preliminary results suggesting that donkey elocution and frequency range may share similarities with African and South American penguins.[1] Penguin speech is notoriously understudied, prolific and expressive. We have spent quality time with several million Adelie, Rockhopper, Macaroni and Chinstrap penguins in the Western Antarctic Peninsula and can attest to their linguistic jamborees, day and night. These speech-fests might well rival the most gossip-rich of all socio-biological clamors.[2]

Like that of penguins and parrots, donkey vocabulary keeps changing: Words become whole paragraphs, uttered in a disorderly eagerness to display intentions with the same verbal proclivity that has infected our greatest senators, poets and rap artists. We all need to communicate. There is so much to say. So much that has not been said before. But, "What?" we ask?

We do not presume to know what is going on. As we've said, despite innumerable encounters with these fantastic beings, we are but novices. We know so very little about them. Sure, we can tell you what we have seen them eat. But, at this sanctuary, we observe nothing of their courtship or their rearing of young because the land they inhabit has a biological carrying capacity that we respect. There is no "horseplay," no breeding here. And so, the range of observable "natural" behavior is reduced. But this doesn't preclude endless expressions of love and friendship. This aggregation of ferocious hoots is no more than the frustrated, desirous, deferred behavior of howling campers eager to party. At the moment, sixty large donkeys compress themselves into the least space possible

to facilitate each equine getting in his or her two cents'
worth while we peculiar, ungainly, bipedal creatures are
available distractions, familiar
curiosities, willing groomers, scratchers
and purveyors of treats.

TALAQUE PAQUE TEAPOT,
CA. 1930S. MEXICO

Present at this love-fest are Silver, Moocee and
Bonnie, who attended our first donkey tea party. On
that memorable day, while Silver licked her plate and licked her
lips, Bonnie and Moocee stuck close, sampling cake and cookies in
the form of biscuits from the picnic table. They demand "tea" each
time we see them. Tea translates to "treat" in donkey parlance. Today, they have innumerable rivals for tea and attention and press
close, ready as ever, to party.

The festivities would go on for hours, weeks, we suspect, because the fascination with one another is endless. What is so fascinating? What are they really feeling, seeing, wanting? What are
we doing? Can we ever know? Does it matter?

Have donkeys fostered their own imaginative notions of us, as
we have of them? A donkey is quick to return kindness and loving
gestures.

They are attracted to us. They seem as naturally curious about
us as we are about them. But what is it that so engages our desire
to know them? Does our fascination with donkeys differ from our
love of playing with a pet dog or cat? Do we need to cuddle, to feel
the warmth of their breath on our face, to stroke their manes, to
remove burrs, to brush from their heads and bodies the dust or
sand in which they love to roll, to clean their eyes and enjoy the

satisfaction they clearly express when we give them acupressure along their backs? Is there a gene or genes within our phenotype that craves expression in behavior that is wild and satisfied only with, by and in the presence of wild creatures other than ourselves? We suspect it is and has always been. It would explain, for example, the plethora of fantastic imagery on those Paleolithic cave walls. This need must be a universal one and was most recently demonstrated by the incredible mothering of an orphaned baby hippo by a hundred-year-old giant male tortoise after both survived a devastating tsunami. They now dwell, loving and inseparable, at Lafarge Park in Kenya.

Every time we stand among these wild donkeys, we are careful. Careful not to put our hands out in a stupid way that might lead to severed fingers or a chunk removed from our wrist. We do not tempt fate by standing behind them, where a single kick to the head could be catastrophic, or, at least, seriously unpleasant. Both are points to keep well in mind before sending your children into the vicinity of donkeys. We do not

DONKEY ACUPRESSURE

wish to convey the notion that these or any other donkeys, mules, hybrids or equines in general can be "trusted" to behave the way we would wish. Any pre-conception or expectation that one is entering the Garden of Eden in the presence of our friends is ill-advised. These are wild creatures. It does not matter that they have been "domesticated" from a thousand breeding intersections. They still retain their wild kick, bite and brains as do cats, in their own way. Donkeys are wild. Mules are wild. Horses are wild. They may walk up to you in a Tibetan meadow, having never laid eyes on a human being before, and put their lips to your lips. Or, they may never let you get within a mile of them.

Years ago, we were on Santa Cruz Island, filming the last sixteen wild horses that roamed there before they were relocated under duress by the park authorities. Those horses had had marginal, perhaps burdensome, experience with people during the previous 150 years, but very little interaction in recent decades. Some of them had had none at all. They would observe hikers from a distance, but that was it. On that day, we approached them slowly, quietly, with only the fondest intentions. They, in turn, ventured

HOPI SACRED CLOWN AND DONKEY. ERNIE FRANKLIN

gingerly up to our small gathering until contact was initiated by both sides to the alliance. A treaty was quickly consummated by their willingness to be stroked, and their own adventure of investigating us. It was a memorable hour in their company, and we like to believe that they felt the same way. It certainly seemed so.

The point is this: we do not understand wildness, except to the extent that we feel it. That is, or should be, enough. When R. B. Townshend visited the Southwest, he learned firsthand about the plight of mules in the desert. Townshend also visited the Perez Family near San Diego, California, reputed to have thousands of equines and the "best" breed of mules in all of North Ameri-

ca. Nonetheless, said Townshend, humans could expect no "love" from these animals who, one must assume, had not taken well to the desert environment. Indeed, Townshend sums it up by conveying the mules' motto: "I'd rather not, and what's more I won't."[3] We know that play is nearly universal in the animal world. We are not alone in gaining pleasure from this. Hence, the anticipation that our joy at being among donkeys is shared by them may be a truism. These donkeys were, after all, rescued, liberated and are adored. Is it a miscalculation to assume they realize and appreciate this?

What is wild in us is wild in them. The equation makes sense though the expression of wildness in the human animal has fortunately been co-opted to various degrees. But, we vent our wildness whenever we can. The great tragedy for the majority of other

species is that we have dominated, confined and exploited them. We have removed much, if not all, of their ability to express their wildness.

To be in the presence of a donkey requires humility, stillness and confidence. They are creatures more ancient than ourselves and worthy of veneration. They don't meet us on neutral ground; the territory is theirs entirely. They are willing to discuss anything. Like so many creatures not human, they forgive us (so long as we observe their defined protocols). They permit us a fresh start. But, we watch our fingers!

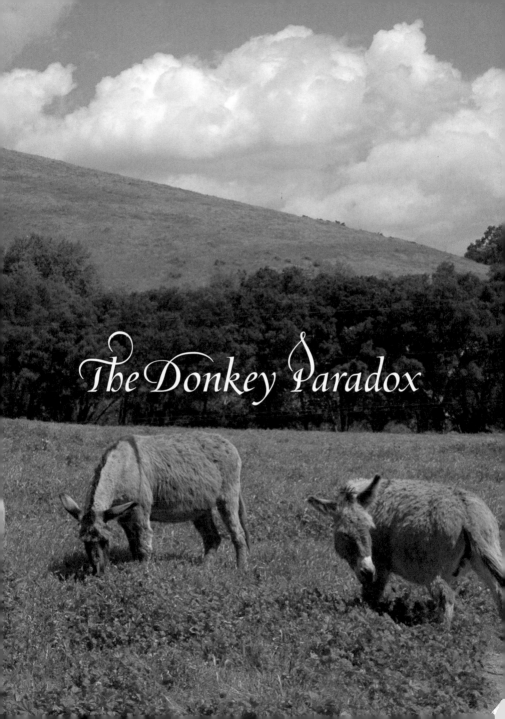

The Donkey Paradox

*I*n this sanctuary where we have been standing all morning, the donkeys graze. Their large schmoozing lips are selectively skimming the natural grasslands, much a mixture of natives and non-natives. When their eating is supplemented with a low crude-fat content diet, it is critical that there be few coarse stems in a hay assemblage that, according to the American Association of Equine Practitioners (AAEP),[1] is about "60% legume content." What is of real concern to those who work with *Equus asinus* is the proper balance between protein and phosphorous, as well as the risk, particularly to geriatric donkeys, of insufficient electrolytes, of their choking and of so-called "digestive upset." Suggestions for food supplements by the AAEP include such things as "sweet, young grass," "soybean meal," "vegetable oil" and "rice bran."[2] These are recommendations for horses, but the similarities to avoid dietary imbalances for donkeys are nearly the same. Any "hot" grass can be a problem. The donkey will ingest too much protein in a short period of time. Chewing is always an issue for older donkeys. Their teeth, which keep growing, require periodic floating (filing) or their ability to eat is impaired, and pain and the potential for serious infection, even death, is an ever-present possibility.

There are fields that donkeys enjoy for the purpose of grazing, rolling about, sidling up to picnic tables, though they enjoy the forest as well. They love the shade, and there is any number of known and unknown factors in dietary favor of their staying to the forests. We think of them as grazers because of their dentition. But, just as wild boars will go frolicking through truffle-rich undergrowth, so, too, donkeys will take advantage, whenever possible, of the nutritious food sources that can be found on or near the forest floor. The forest offers innumerable scratching posts, as well. It's just that most people have only witnessed donkeys out in the open.

Donkeys are extraordinarily complicated. They are no different in that respect than we. But, our understanding of their needs is more challenged than one might think. When a grandparent cries out "Help!" the alarm bell is unambiguous. When a parent shouts, it says one thing. When a child panics, or weeps, it says another. Do we know, for certain, what a donkey sounds like when he cries? Can we distinguish cries? Do we know one bray from another? And, speaking of braying, what on earth was on the mind of that donkey who commenced his ballyhoo at an impromptu sermon of St. Francis? Was he merely praying? Whatever was the case, it is legend or history that when the holy brother asked his donkey brother to hold off and let him get a word in, the donkey promptly obliged.[3]

Whatever their inspiration, we must pay attention to our friends' words. There are countless concerns to deftly navigate, keeping any shepherd of donkeys on top of the subtle or not so subtle. Here are a few examples: manure disposition, direction of shelters, sand pile configuration, size of pasture, degree of hill slope, number of animals on a given acre, predators, food competition, weather variation, humidity and temperature change in any 24-hour period; plus, soil type, invasive weeds and poisonous plants. There are also issues of relationship and personality, such as loneliness, simmering competition among certain animals to-

wards each other, and the needs of "gifted children," melancholic
mothers, alienated fathers and rival siblings. These last three are
not issues at this sanctuary given the zero-population growth principle here embraced. But, what of the possibility of boredom, frustration, anger or jealousy? What are the causes and consequences
of an existentialist disposition in a certain donkey? What about
loners, those with congenital defects, the mentally challenged, the
particularly wild or restive? The poets and dreamers; those who
simply will not touch anything but carrots? Think of parliament
or grammar school or any of the individual dynamics in separate
households—histories, tangles, forlorn hopes, joys—and multi-
ply all that by the genetic drift that has defined a new species, and
you approach the neighborhood of *donkeyville*!

Delightful donkeyville delinquents are Al Capone and Pushy.

They share a passion for naughtiness or, as we have come to understand it as a result of thoroughly noisy indoctrination, "personal initiative."

Al Capone is a clever boy with a penchant for mischief. He is a beautiful scarface and a thief. He likes to help himself to whatever happens to take his fancy. Al can be seen climbing the steps of the storage barn and raiding it for anyone's grub since he particularly likes to steal food, insisting stolen food tastes best.

Pushy likes to stroll up the steps of the ranch house, wander into the kitchen and open the refrigerator door. He usually manages to make off with carrots, apples or whatever else he can get in his mouth.

Pushy loves to do just that: push. He nudges. He nestles. He rests his head on our shoulders. But, mainly, he buries his muzzle in one back or another and exerts loving, insistent pressure. His exuberant affection never offends.

Pushy and Al Capone are two of our unselfconscious mentors. They, along with Lucy, Boxer, Bono and Roo, Maii and Elayne give us lessons in patience and virtue. We slowly inch our way toward understanding, thinking we'll never get there.

Yet, we are so close to what we dream of as comprehension. We can feel it; nearly, touch it. There are some donkeys one would think had actually tutored Eddie Murphy for his brilliant performance in the movie *Shrek* and its sequel and the whole artistic team that made the donkey in those films so remarkable. One wonders what Caravaggio would have thought of the donkey in *Shrek*? He probably would have drawn great inspiration from that donkey extraordinaire. But there are other donkeys who clearly withhold ev-

erything. Bringing them "out" requires patience. Sometimes, that means simply standing in one place, quietly, head down, for ten, fifteen minutes, longer. Eventually, they will come to you. Stand there long enough and they will sometimes proffer a protective shield around you, several donkeys at once joining in to see what is wrong.

Donkeys are quick studies. They may well get agitated, socially speaking, and this might have to do with a concern that someone else will be first to be scratched or get the treat. And that jealousy, given their numbers, is not unreasonable. To the aggressive and near-to-hand go the spoils. But it appears clear, as well, that they feel altruistic concern for us. Love is not far behind. Love from a circle of donkeys that surround us, trust us and await the demonstration of our reciprocity is heaven. And, it's scary. From our

field studies, we observe that they want to share their love with us. More than once, each of us has stood or sat and felt the palpable weight of a donkey chin resting on a shoulder. Or, we have felt the gentle pressure as a donkey forehead pressed against a back, an arm, our side. Or, felt the tugging on a shirt or jacket as a donkey picked a pocket. Or, felt the hot breath of a donkey investigating with great lips some part of ourselves or our gear.

Holmes is chief investigator, sniffer, pickpocket and engineer. He manages to maintain his dignity while going about his avocation. He is so beautiful, so Platero-like in appearance if not modesty, that we are never offended by his activities. He has dissected more than one hat. He is admirable and inspired. Perhaps he is bored and we are a diversion. When the grasses are green, he keeps his nose down, busy with real business: Eating. If he could dine si-

multaneously in two fields while daintily demolishing carrots on the side, we imagine he would.

From our experience we do not confirm the theory expounded in the famed "Buridan's Ass" syndrome, named after a fourteenth century French philosopher, Jean Buridan who studied a canine paradox referred to by Aristotle in his work *De Caelo*. The syndrome refers to a scenario, envisioned by Buridan where a donkey agonized over two possible meals, each a bundle of hay sitting on the ground equidistant from the animal. Unable to choose between the two equally inviting dinners, the donkey, theoretically, starved to death. This is preposterous. We believe the donkey would have eaten both bundles! But a different explanation was offered for the unexpected behavior that one donkey displayed in the history of a Franciscan saint known as a miracle worker. Earlier, we re-

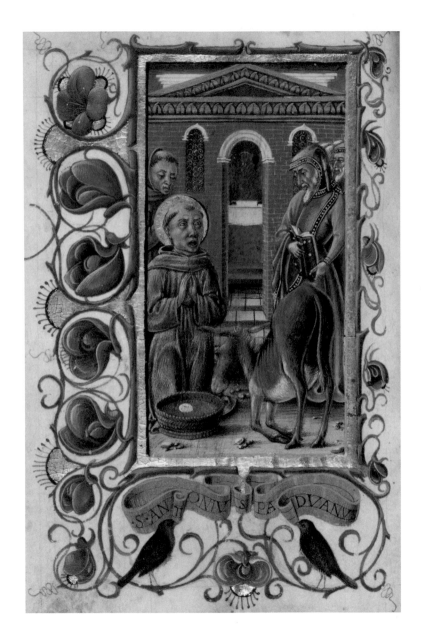

ferred to the painting by Beccafumi in which a mule or donkey kneels before Saint Anthony. The donkey knelt in devotion at the Saint's behest. As described by Kurt Barstow in his commentary on *Saint Anthony of Padua* painted by Taddeo Crivelli, in order to convert heretics, St. Anthony persuaded a donkey, after three days of abstinence from food or water, to kneel down and venerate the host rather than indulge in a generous meal of hay. The donkey complied, and the heretics vowed to embrace Christianity.[4]

During the Middle Ages, philosophers developed a term for ambiguous but puzzling arguments or explanations, apparently clever, but flawed and intended to deceive: sophisms. These cloaked riddles were more about manipulating language than describing conceptual problems inherent to human nature or perception. Two classic case studies involved the donkey: "Every man sees a donkey" and "All men are donkeys or men and donkeys are donkeys."[5] In yet another version of what we would term the alleged "donkey-bind," researchers looking at learning mechanisms in patients afflicted with Parkinson's disease have referred to a motivational learning theory known as "carrot and stick," which is based upon the notion of training a donkey with positive or negative reinforcement.[6] Somehow, despite countless examples to the contrary, the donkey has been viewed as an emblem of stubbornness and stupidity. The opposite is true, of course, of these noble creatures. The word "stupid" is a human invention, inapplicable to the living world. No creature suffers for lack of intelligence. All beings confirm their brilliance by their very existence. The story from the *Torah* of the

{169}

SCENE DEPICTING THE MIRACLE OF THE DONKEY,
SAINT ANTHONY OF PADUA, TADDEO CRIVELLI, CA. 1469

donkey and Balaam, the emissary of the Moabite King Balak, demonstrates clearly that the donkey is loyal, wise, self-sacrificing and god-like, such that the so-called "donkey mouth" referenced in the Mishna is considered to be one of the "ten unique things created at dusk on the sixth day of creation." The Jewish explanation concerns the ancient Hebraic words for donkey (*chamor*), jennet (*osson*) and mule (*pered*). All are viewed as aspects of the human personali-

ty, religious temperament and moral responsibility.

In Brazil, there are said to be something on the order of one hundred Portuguese words for donkey, all "affectionate."[7] In ancient Israel, even if one's enemy was riding a donkey, if that donkey was "overburdened" you had a moral obligation to assist it. Indeed, the donkey provided an ethical mirror for human beings.[8] Hence, apparent ancient Hebrew insistence on animal rights: "An animal's suffering must be relieved" (Deuteronomy 12:4) and "A person must feed his animals before himself" (Deuteronomy 11:15).[9] The donkey, in other words, is a critical being in Hebrew tradition. In addition, ancient Judaic law insisted that just as a human should have the Sabbath as a day of rest, so should a donkey (Exodus 23:12; Deuteronomy 5:14).[10]

The late Roman Catholic Priest, Father Antonio Vieira, a world expert on donkeys and one of their greatest champions from Brazil, declared that the animal is referenced at least 220 times in the Bible. Life is hard for the poor in Brazil, but the donkey's life is harder. As Padre Vieria recounts in his seminal work, *Our Brother, the Donkey,* "Nobody today feels, like Ishmael, son of Abraham, happy and honored to be called 'Ass,' not even by an angel. Instead we constantly say, 'I lead a donkey's life, I work like a mule, I suffer like a blind man's donkey.'"[11] In Brazil, a donkey can be pur-

NATIVITY. MELCHOIR BROEDERLAM, CA. 1400

chased for a dollar (a chicken for $3 dollars). Animal rights activists stopped the trade in donkey meat within Brazil and today donkeys may number as many as 2 million but are, sadly, perceived as a collective burden on the country.[12]

The donkey paradox persists to this day. They suffer in Brazil and are sold at auction for dog meat in the U.S. Notwithstanding such nonfiction horror tales, countless other more fortunate donkeys throughout the world are loved and cared for—some as pets, many in sanctuaries where they are able to express their wildness.

Film director Viktor Petkov has a donkey tell his own story as a Shakespearian soliloquy[13] and the great writer Nikos Kazantzakis speaks of the donkey as that fellow being within who carries our soul on this earth. There are the Persian tales of Nasreddin Hoja who travels the world with his amusing companion donkey[14] and the great Medieval Sufi mystic poet Jalal al din Rumi (1207–1273) who spoke of the ass as a great Gnostic, capable—as in Jewish tradition—of seeing God.

The Genius of Donkeys

*A*nd so we must ask, what of the future welfare of donkeys? Fortunately, there are an increasing number of donkey sanctuaries and a number of caring scientists specializing in their wellbeing. Patricia D. Moehlman has proposed steps that could better ensure proper and appropriate aid for the "Critically Endangered" sub-species *Equus africanus, E. a. africanus* and the sub-species *E. a. somaliensis* in Somalia, Ethiopia and Eritrea.[1] In North America, a brilliant argument has been made by one of the longtime leaders in the realm of wildlife immuno-contraception. Dr. Jay F. Kirkpatrick, Director of The Science and Conservation Center in Billings, Montana, has suggested the reclassification of the whole remarkable genus *Equus* in such a manner that it would once again be perceived as a truly wild native species to this continent, as once it was, prior to dispersal to Eurasia sometime between 2 and 3.9 million years ago.[2] Kirkpatrick and Fazio's argument is compelling. They point out that once there were twenty-seven different genera of equines. Today, throughout the world, only one is left, which includes donkeys and horses and zebras and all of their hybrid varieties and breeds. When the last of the huge glaciations scoured North America some eleven thousand to thirteen thousand years ago, there were massive extinctions. One of the most recent known equine extinctions occurred in 1880. That was the tarpan (*Equus ferus ferus*) with no gene surviving, although the Tierpark Hellabrunn (Munich Zoo) and the Berlin Zoo were able to breed a Konik (Wild Polish Horse) that re-

sembles the tarpan in terms of conformation.[3] Fortunately for the one remaining equine genus, migrations had occurred during the previous few million years to Asia. Otherwise, there would be no donkeys or horses anywhere on the planet. Columbus, during his "second voyage" in 1493, brought Spanish horses with him, according to Kirkpatrick and Fazio, first to the Virgin Islands and then to Mexico. Most intriguingly of all, the authors point out that recent DNA markers show that today's horse, *Equus caballus*, is genetically the same as *Equus lambei* which was possibly the last equine to go extinct in North America. This means that today's horse is very likely a North American endemic, just as donkeys appear endemic in parts of Africa and Tibet.

There has been talk recently of the "rewilding of America."[4] Not simply by the reintroduction of more wolves or lynx or bison, but also by the introduction of lions, cheetahs, camels and elephants to the tall-grass prairies of this continent. The idea is to populate the nation with species similar to those that roamed these lands freely in the Pleistocene era: mammoths, saber-tooth tigers, and native North American equids, among others. What was once incredibly wild, would be wild again, hence "re-wilding." The Cornell evolutionary biologist Dr. Josh Donlan, principle author of the provocative research paper published in *Nature* magazine, writes, "Horses and camels originated in North America, and many species were present in the Late Pleistocene. Feral horses (*Equus caballus*) and asses (*E. asinus*), widely viewed as pests in the United States, are plausible proxies for extinct American species. Also, given that most of the surviving Eurasian and African species are now critically endangered, establishing Asian asses (*E. hemionus*) and Przewalski's horses (*E. przewalskii*) in North America might help prevent the extinction of these endangered species and would restore equid species to their evolutionary homeland." [5]

Fortunately for all of us, a few wild equines still exist out there, but their numbers are declining. They need help. The Bureau of Land Management has something like "40,000 horses and 5,000 burros roaming 17.4 million acres of public and private lands," according to the Wild Horse Foundation,[6] which has also published data to the effect that mustangs graze approximately twelve hours per day, consuming on average eleven kilograms of food. Proportionate numbers might be extrapolated for feral donkeys. The problem is not only the donkeys' healthy population growth rate, estimated at between seventeen percent and twenty-five percent per year, in good years, but the fact of the negative bias promulgated by most government agencies and ranchers. Some thirty thousand ranching enterprises in a dozen Western states argue that these splendid equines are exerting undue competitive pressure for scarce food and water resources (an estimated six thousand pounds of herbs, grass and other browse per animal per year) on forage lands needed by cattle, while government officials constantly complain of wild equine decimation of native plant populations.

This alleged conflict, if scrutinized, is clearly tragic. It has resulted in government roundups of burros and horses and the repeated attempts by profiteers to sell wild equines: A "1,000 pound mustang can bring $700 to $900 at a slaughter house," [7] and that meat is much favored by self-styled gourmands across Europe and Japan. Ironically, the cost to taxpayers for subsidizing this slaughter is huge. The alternative of simply letting the feral equines be,

or, at least, providing sanctuaries for them, has been economically assessed by the Center for Biological Diversity in Tucson, Arizona. The costs/benefits are clear and overwhelmingly favor letting the equines roam wild and free in sanctuaries carved out of existing Bureau of Land Management, Forest Service or National Park lands. Many Americans are being deceived about the true status of the wild equine, while the ecological integrity of the U.S. outback continues to be compromised—not by wild horses and burros, but by over four million cows. [8]

The U.S. Humane Society reports that ninety thousand equines, a significant percentage of which is comprised of *Equus*

asinus, are killed in the U.S. each year and that previous "owners are often totally unaware of the pain, fear and suffering their
horses endure before being slaughtered."[9]

In addition, another serious problem, genetic variability, con-
fronts American-based equines. According to Gus Cothran, of
the University of Kentucky, "long-term genetic viability" among
equine herds requires at least 150 individuals. However, something
like seventy-five percent of the 209 BLM herds have fewer numbers than that.[10]

Throughout the world ecological arguments for the preservation and protection of wild equines abound, but greater forces are
at work to negate the animals' futures. Across Africa, food and
labor issues continue to cause difficulties. In Nigeria, the most

DONKEYS, 1829. MOON, GRAVES & BOYS, LONDON

populous nation in Africa, most of the 800,000 donkeys are "used for carrying loads" with harnesses that are largely inappropriate. In the Sudan, where the U.N. Food and Agriculture Organization strives to ameliorate the ravages of famine, donkey health has been impaired from protracted drought and lack of veterinary supplies. This decline of donkey health has furthered the stress on impoverished, donkey-dependent communities, particularly in the country's western, war-engulfed Darfur region. Darfur is representative of many parts of Africa that are resource bereft, places where donkeys can make the difference between life and death. And, as of January 2006, millions of people across northern Africa were facing starvation and many were dependent on equines for food. No one knows how many equines are also at risk, but one corre-

spondent for the BBC was reported as saying that "in northern Kenya...corpses of cattle and donkeys are lying everywhere."[11]

In China, another problem faces donkeys: genetic deterioration among breeds which prompted an "urgent" call by scientists "to protect the genetic resources of (the) Chinese donkey" whose origins were recently discovered to be African.[12] Tibetan asses are supposedly not endangered. In fact, in some of the Chinese National Parks within Tibet, there are claims made that the animals have far exceeded their carrying capacity, their ecologically sustainable numbers. There has been some talk among the Chinese authorities of culling thousands of them.[13]

A very different situation exists in Mexico, England and Ireland where donkeys have a brighter prospect, as do people. Genetic research on Mexican donkey breeds suggests high genetic diversity on account of the mixed, vibrant derivations, namely, Andaluzan, Zamorano-Leonesa and Majorera (the Canary Island donkey populations). This combination has resulted in what is known as the Creole breed of Mexican donkey, one that has Spanish and African blood and is well distributed throughout Mexico.[14]

In Europe, as in North America, a very different vision for twenty-first century donkey conservation has emerged, in view of the extinction context. It is understood that the current landscapes of Europe were fashioned, in part, by herbivores, plant eating species, many of them from equine genera that are all now extinct and whose niches go unoccupied. This presents a formidable opportunity for the re-introduction of feral donkeys and horses, as well as wild cattle who would, in essence, re-fill or mimic the niches once occupied by the now extinct *Bos primigenius,* the Eurasian aurochs seen in the form of bulls in so many of the Paleolithic cave paintings.[15] We can only imagine the potential ecological benefits of such initiatives.

Interbreeding and genetic attenuation have become a major world-wide crisis, despite some islands of remaining genetic vitality. In 2005, the U.N. Food and Agriculture Organization published its Domestic Animal Diversity list suggesting that, of the known 4,000 mammalian and bird breeds, approximately a third were "at high risk" with vulnerable horse breeds at the highest risk of all. We would urge all those concerned with the one known surviving genus of equines in the world to recognize donkeys—regardless of breed—as being vulnerable.[16] These animals are genetically, emotionally, ecologically and psychologically at risk.

IN THE SNOW, DONKEY SANCTUARY, UK

In England, an archaeological discovery of a highly significant donkey skeleton may change the donkey's place in that country's history. According to Archaeological Solutions Ltd., "the first confirmed Anglo Saxon donkey in London" was found recently at Dean's Yard, Westminster School near Westminster Abbey, at a World Heritage Site excavation of medieval structures. There, with the enhancement by radiocarbon technology, an eighth to nineth century donkey skeleton was uncovered. It is the first of its kind found from the "Medieval Period" in England.[17] The attention paid to it, in the precious context of very few donkey bones having ever been found in the U.K., argues that a special World Heritage status be conferred upon donkeys in England.

In Egypt, a similar cultural renaissance favoring donkeys could be advocated on the basis of historical associations. Egyptian tombs from the Fourth Dynasty (ca. 2675–2565 BC) suggest that burial with donkeys was considered a status symbol and the "elite" of the period might own as many as a thousand donkeys per family.[18] Even earlier, in Sumeria, there is ample evidence for the cross-breeding and domestication of donkeys, and the "half-ass or hemione." In addition, the translations of ancient Sumerian cuneiform tablets make it clear that domestic asses, onagers and various hybrids were identified and distinguished. *Equus asinus* was known as anse.[19]

In Greece, donkeys have been critical to monastic life and to the eco-tourist trade. Equines, in general, were always beloved in Greece starting with Alexander the Great's horse, Bucephalus. Google "donkeys and Greek monasteries" and you are likely to find over 53,000 references. That's because there is virtually no mountain monastery and no traditional village where donkeys do not have their own history and are not deeply involved with human culture. Greek carnivals, Saints Days, celebrations and blessings of every kind tend to involve donkeys. Sheep and goats are also integral to Greek culture, and throughout the world there is little surprise at the fact donkeys are often regarded as the protectors, or patron saints of these smaller cud-chewing herbivores.

There is also a specific critical ancient Greek connection to donkeys—to equines in general—that merits special mention as it emerges in parallel with the earliest democratic instincts and some of the greatest art and enlightened thinking in human history. Michael Ventris (1922–1956) was the brilliant decipherer of Linear B, the so-called Minoan Script dated between 1750 and 1450 BC. The stone entablatures on which the script was discovered were first found at the

BRUCE ON THERA, 1968

Palace of Knossos on Crete by Arthur Evans in 1900. They bore pictograms of four horse heads, allegedly two horses and two foals. The English word "foal" derives from the Greek word, *polos*. What cannot be ascertained is whether the "foals" are actually donkeys. They may be, and that would make Linear B the earliest European language to acknowledge donkeys in pictographic form.[20]

On Aegean islands like Hydra, where there are few roads, donkeys have provided traditional access, not only to Profitis Llias Monastery on the highest mountain above town, but for general non-pedestrian travel on the island. There are donkey trails

FIRST TIME OUT, DONKEY SANCTUARY, UK

throughout Greece. The ubiquitous image of the donkey makes it the virtual iconic species of the country. At every port, the donkeys are there. When Prince Charles made his third private visit recently to the ancient Mount Athos complex, he came to the Vatopedhiou Monastery with some "thirty cases of gear" carried up the old donkey trails.[21] The Donkey Sanctuary in Great Britain has expressed concern about the abuse of donkeys used as human "taxis" in countries like Greece and Spain and has published a checklist for tourists who can make their own informed decisions on whether or not to impose themselves upon a donkey, particularly in 100-degree heat. The list consists of such donkey basics as food and water, shelter or shade, a harness that does not cause wounds, and attention to the donkey's apparent health, happiness and well-being.[22]

SKY AND MUM, DONKEY SANCTUARY, UK

One key to the future of donkeys is clearly going to come from the public support for sanctuaries, whether they are on private or public lands. Public lands would require agency representatives and biologists to recognize the role donkeys have in what has been earlier referred to as a "re-wilding" benefit to all Americans; donkeys co-existing with native plants, bighorn sheep, pronghorn antelope, bison, wolves, bobcats and others. On private lands, the donkey sanctuaries throughout the world provide safe havens for these magical creatures: oases of trust and love where humans may ensure that donkeys remain a living testament to the possibilities for harmony on earth. There is so much for us to learn from these all-abiding creatures, these living, dreaming sources of profound meditation.

The Donkey Sanctuary in Devon is particularly noteworthy because of the large number of equines that are protected there. Next to the town of Sidmouth, the sanctuary has over nine thousand donkeys. On March 16, 2004, Grumps gave birth to Ponk, a donkey foal who was the 9000th member of the equine community there. In strolling through the sanctuary the first and most lasting impression is that of collaborative joy between donkeys and the many human caregivers and visitors. Set in gorgeous countryside with lush grass, if ever there appeared a kind of interspecies utopia, it is the Donkey Sanctuary. This piece of paradise is surely a fitting emblem for the entire international sanctuary movement that has strived so hard to adopt donkeys, liberate them, and confer upon them unstinting love.

In that spirit, we list at the end of this book some of the important donkey sanctuaries with the hope that people will do whatever they can to assist these many inspired efforts to restore to the world the poetic balance that only the continued existence and happiness of donkeys can truly ensure.[23]

Donkeys deserve the best that humanity is capable of providing.

In many respects, we have learned that among donkeys we are each of us capable of discovering some new trait or insight never before commented upon, or even observed. Ecopoetic field studies are their own science, where every anecdote and subjective impression becomes critical evidence in the accumulation of experiences toward some new science. Donkeys can help us because there is shared love. They are, in their own right, after so many thousands of years in human company, experts at interspecies mingling. If humans will only learn how to listen, make the effort and encourage them with our trust and love. Then, we are certain, there will be endless encyclopedias' worth of knowledge and spiritual insight opened to us. We humans need only to be attuned, to listen, to be still.

And it may well be that what donkeys have to teach us is crucial to our own survival as a species.

The day draws to a close. We have been with one loving, furry-eared friend and her fractious companion since early morning. Most of the others have wandered off, over a ridge. But these two have stayed behind to "hang" with us.

As we talk of our proposed drive home, both donkeys have their enormous heads on our shoulders, listening intently, their eyes

sparkling. It's as close, we imagine, as we'll ever get to Paradise. Our hearts are full. Whatever undeciphered or undecipherable thoughts, daydreams or musings occupy our friends, our gratitude for their permission to come near is boundless.

Curious, elusive, loving and mysterious donkeys, each of you is an individual of such depth and feeling. Our journey to know you may be unending. Our love for you is full, present and unequivocal. Thank you for this magical day.

Notes

First Impressions

1   See the lovely story of Richard Alexander Henderson in Glyn Harper, *The Donkey Man*, illustrated by Bruce Potter. Auckland, New Zealand: Reed Publishing, 2004.

2   Roger Blench, *The History and Spread of Donkeys in Africa*, London: Overseas Development Institute. 2000.

Paul Starkey and Denis Fielding (eds.), *Donkeys, People and Development A Resource Book of the Animal Traction Network for Eastern and Southern Africa (ATNESA)*. Wageningen, The Netherlands, ACP-EU Technical Centre for Agricultural and Rural Cooperation (CTA), 2004. pp. 22–30. See www.atnesa. org.

Along with the African Wild Ass, there is also the Asiatic Wild Ass or Onager, the Tibetan Wild Ass, or Kiang, and four other wild equids, namely: Grevy's Zebra, the Mountain Zebra, the Plains Zebra and Przewalski's Horse. See Dr. Patricia D. Moehlman and Anna Knee, "Urgent Action Needed for Conservation of Wild Equids," Gland, Switzerland: *IUCN (The World Conservation Union)*, January 27, 2003. See www.iucn.org/themes/ssc/ actionplans/equids/equidap.htm.

3   Paul Starkey and Malcolm Starkey, "Regional and world trends in donkey populations." Starkey and Fielding (eds.), *Donkeys, People and Development*, Animal Traction Network for Eastern and Southern Africa, Wageningen, The Netherlands, 2004, p.10, www.atnesa.org/donkeyspeopledevelopment. htm.

4   Myra Cohn Livingston and Joseph F. Dominguez Translation of "Passing of the Ducks," Juan Ramon Jimenez, *Platero y yo*, (*Platero and I*), Illustrations by Antonio Frasconi, New York: Clarion Books, 1994.

On a Winter's Morning

1   See website for information on the donkey: Alberta Government, "Ropin' the Web," Agriculture, Food and Rural Development, November 1990. See Agdex467/20-1 at http://www1.agric.gov.ab.ca/$department/deptdocs.nsf/all/ agdex598.

2   Svendsen has subsequently affected the rescue of nearly twelve thousand other donkeys. She oversees ten sanctuary farms in the U.K. and Ireland; and has programs in many other countries. The Donkey Sanctuary, headquartered in Devon, constitutes the largest donkey sanctuary in the world and provides a window both on the urgent need of donkeys for

assistance and understanding, as well as the capacity of the human spirit to respond. See www.thedonkeysanctuary.org.uk.

3   Other writers and illustrators have expressed a love of, or fascination with, donkeys by using them as metaphors, fellow journeyers and explorers, and a means of intimate self-expression. Among the many examples are E. Pitcher Woodward, *On A Donkey's Hurricane Deck: A Tempestuous Voyage of Four Thousand Ninety-Six Miles Across the American Continent On A Burro in 340 Days and 2 Hours*, New York: I. H. Blanchard, 1902; Roger Duvoisin, *Donkey-Donkey: the troubles of a silly little donkey*, Racine: Whitman Publishing Company, 1933; Cormac Breathnach, translated from the Irish by Padraig O"Conaire, illustrated by Michael O"Liammoir, *Field & Fare: Travels With A Donkey In Ireland*, Dublin: The Talbot Press, 1930; Adam Pio and Lori Anderson, *The Magic Donkey*, Milwaukee: Raintree, 1990; Margaret Wise Brown, illustrated by Ashley Wolff, *Little Donkey Close Your Eyes*, New York: HarperCollins, 1995; H. E. Bates, *Achilles the Donkey*, Eau Clair, Wisconsin: E. M. Hale and Company, 1962; Clyde Robert Bulla, illustrated by Lois Lenski, *The Donkey Cart*, New York: Thomas Y. Cromwell, 1946; Enid Blyton, *The Clever Little Donkey*, London: William Collins, 1956; Terry Southern (Text) and Larry Rivers (Illustrations), *The Donkey and the Darling*, A Portfolio of 52 Lithographs, U.L.A.E./Universal Limited Art Editions, 1976; Barbara Helen Berger, *The Donkey's Dream*, New York: Philomel Books, 1985; Miodrag Bulatovic, *A Hero On A Donkey*, London: Secker Warburg, 1966; Ludwig Bemelmans, *Donkey Inside*, New York: Viking, 1941; and Patricia Lynch, illustrated by Jack B. Yeats, *The Turf-Cutter's Donkey: An Irish Story of Mystery & Adventure*, London: J. M. Dent & Sons, 1934.

4   A brief introduction to the evolution of equines can be found in *Wikipedia*, the superb free encyclopedia, www.wikipedia.org.

5   See Sue M. McDonnell, "Reproductive behavior of donkeys (*Equus asinus*)," *Applied Animal Behavior Science* 60, 1998, pp. 277-282. In figure 2 of her essay, McDonnell shows an image of more than a half-dozen jennies, standing around a single resting jack and writes, "When the jack is teasing or breeding one jenny, the others in the sexually active group cluster near the mating pair, often with a burst of sexual interaction among the jennies" p. 279. There is an apparently high level of sexual exuberance amongst donkeys.

6   See M. Henry, L. D. Lodi, and M. M. F. O. Gastal, "Sexual behaviour of domesticated donkeys (*Equus asinus*) breeding under controlled or free range management systems," *Applied Animal Behaviour Science*, Vol. 60, Issues 2-3, November 1998, pp. 263-276.

7   See "Feral horse (*Equus caballus*) and feral donkey (*Equus asinus*)," *Australian Government, Department of the Environment and Heritage*, 2004. www.deh.gov.au.

8   See Patricia D. Moehlman, Lynn E. Fowler and John H. Roe, "Feral asses (*Equus africanus*) of Volcano Alcedo, Galapagos: behavioral ecology, spatial distribution, and social organization," *Applied Animal Behaviour Science*, *Vol.* 60, Issues 2-3, November 15, 1998, pp. 197-210. See also Patricia D. Moehlman, "Feral asses (*Equus africanus*): Intraspecific variation in social organization in arid and mesic habitats," *Applied Animal Behaviour Science*, *Vol.* 60, Issues 2-3, November 15, 1998, pp. 171-195. {Mesic: prarie, full sun exposure, deep, loamy soils}.

9   See www.ultimateungulate.com/Perissodactyla/Equus_asinus.html.

Approaching a Donkey

1   See: P. Myers, R. Espinosa, C. S. Parr, T. Jones, G. S. Hammond, and T. A. Dewey, *The Animal Diversity Web*, 2006: http://animaldiversity.org: http://animaldiversity.ummz.umich.edu/site/accounts/classification/path/Equus_asinus.html. See also: *NODC Taxonomic Code, database version* 8.0, 1996, and *Mammal Species of the World*, 1998 http://nmnhgoph.si.edu/msw/Equus asinus.

2   Neither the fact that Borax-trundling mule teams were sent vastly overburdened throughout Death Valley in the 1880s, nor that they were dispatched to the blizzardy Antarctic in the spring of 1912 to attempt a rescue of explorer Robert Falcon Scott, implies that this species has any special fondness for such environments.

3   E. A. Canacoo and F. K. Avornyo, "Daytime activities of donkeys at range in the coastal savanna of Ghana," *Applied Animal Behaviour Science*, *Vol.* 60, Issues 2-3, November 1998, pp. 229-234.

4   See Patricia D. Moehlman, "Behavioral patterns and communication in feral asses (*Equus africanus*)," *Applied Animal Behavior Science*, *Volume* 60, Issues 2-3, November 15, pp. 125-169. Also see, Rebecca Rudman, "The social organization of feral donkeys (*Equus asinus*) on a small Caribbean island (St. John, U.S. Virgin Islands)," *Applied Animal Behaviour Science*, *Volume* 60, Issues 2-3, November 15, 1998, pp. 211-228.

5   Rudman, *ibid.*

6   Vicki Knotts Abbott, "Donkey Training: Part One," p. 1, 2001 at www.donkeymuleinfo.com/Donkey%20Training%20E-Clinic%20Part%201.htm.

The Infinity of Natural History

1   P. J. Mueller, P. Protos, K. A. Houpt, and P. J. Van Soest, "Chewing behaviour in the domestic donkey (Equus asinus) fed fibrous forage," *Applied Animal Behaviour Science*, Vol. 60, Issues 2–3, November 15, 1998, pp. 241–251.

2   www.donkeybreedsociety.co.uk/Page.aspx?TagName=AboutDonkeys.

3   See John Hauer, "The Natural Superiority of the Mule or, Why Uncle Mule Can Out-jump Your Horse," *Saturday Evening Post*, March 2001. See also, John Hauer, (Sena Hauer, ed.), *The Natural Superiority of Mules*, Guilford, Connecticut: The Lyons Press, 2005.

4   *Ibid.*

5   Frank Gilbert Roe, *The Indian and the Horse*, Norman, OK: University of Oklahoma Press, 1955, pp. 270, 276; Cited from *Lewis & Clark's Journals*, Vol. III, p. 28 (ed. by Thwaites), and Vol. II, p. 547 (ed. by Coves).

6   *Ibid.*, John Hauer, who cites this telling quote by Lincoln. The Civil War also harbored insights into the importance placed upon mules by all concerned. The phrase "40 acres and a mule" was supposedly the boon held out by the U.S. Government to each freed slave (although there is little formal documentation to support this). And when General Robert E. Lee and his army were defeated by General Ulysses S. Grant on April 9, 1865, Grant permitted the Confederate soldiers to hold on to their mules and horses (and guns). See www.historyplace.com/civilwar/index.html.

7   See A. K. Thiemann and N. J. Bell, "The Peculiarities of Donkey Respiratory Disease," The Donkey Sanctuary, Sidmouth, Devon in P. Lekeux, (ed.) *Equine Respiratory Diseases*, Ithica, New York: International Veterinary Information Service (www.ivis.org), 2001. See also Animal Welfare Board of India; www.awbi.org/pamp7.htm.

8   See "Donkey Care," www.farmanimalshelters.org/care_donkey.htm.

9   See "Laminitis," www.homeofrestforhorses.co.uk/laminitis.html; See also, John Hauer, (Sena Hauer, ed.), *The Natural Superiority of Mules*, Guilford, Connecticut: The Lyons Press, 2005, pp. 12–13.

10 See the Oklahoma State University Board of Regents, "Breeds of Livestock," 2003, which cites I. L. Mason, *A World Dictionary of Livestock Breeds, Types and Varieties*, Fourth Edition, C.A.B. International, 1996, at www.ansi. okstate.edu/breeds/other/donkey/.

11 See B. V. E. Segwagwe, A. A. Aganga and C. Patrick, "Investigation into the Common Diseases of Donkeys (*Equus asinus*) in Botswana," Proceedings of an ATNESA Workshop, South Africa, September 1999.

12 See the Selected Publications of Professor Itzhak Choshniak, who has

researched all of these various biochemical and physiological qualities of the desert ruminants and non-ruminants (e.g., donkeys: animals with a stomach, intestines and caecum, but no rumen), in such papers as (with H. Israely), "Energy-Metabolism and Digestibility in Donkeys Fed Low Quality Food," *Israel Journal of Zoology*, 33, 116, 1985; and, (with H. Israely and A. Brosh), "Physiological Characteristics That Help Goats and Donkeys to Cope with the Nitrogen Shortage in Desert Forage,"*Israel Journal of Zoology*, 34, 97, 1987.

13 See also, the work of Fall Brayer of the American Donkey and Mule Society, Inc., in Lewisville, Texas, 1995; and N. G. Dmitriez and L. K. Ernst, "Animal Genetic Resources of the USSR," Animal Production and Health Paper, Food and Agriculture Organization of the United Nations, 1989. For the five Spanish breeds, see Jose Aranguren-Mendez, Jordi Jordana and Mariano Gomez, "Genetic diversity in Spanish donkey breeds using microsatellite DNA markers," *Genetics Selection Evolution*, 33, 2001, pp. 433–442. at: www.edpsciences.org/articles/gse/abs/2001/04/g330405/g330405.html.

14 The Sharja Donkey Project, funded by the German Research Foundation (DFG); See the Ernst-Moritz-Arndt University - Greifswald Zoological Institute and Museum, "Functional morphology, Ecology and Evolutionary Biology of Terrestrial Mammals research projects" by PD Dr. Thomas M. Kaiser, http://www.evolution.uni-greifswald.de/eng/1.php.

15 See Society for Animal Protection (a division of the Animal Welfare Institute), www.saplonline.org, May 18, 2006 Press Release: "Wild Horses Again Win Victory in U.S. House of Representatives," regarding America's wild, free-roaming horses and burros.

16 See The American Livestock Breeds Conservancy, in Pittsboro, North Carolina: albe@albe-usa.org.

17 See www.imh.org/imh/bw/donkey.html.

18 See www.lovelongears.com/zorse.html.

19 Colin P. Groves, "Taxonomy of Living Equidae," Chapter 8, p. 96, in *Equid Biology and Ecology*, www.icun.org/themes/ssc/ sgs/equid/docs/part3chapter8.pdf.

20 George Torode speaking in"Guernsey Donkeys –A born and bred Guernseyman is generally referred to as 'Donkey' –but why?" *The Guernsey Press and Star*, April 6, 2006.

21 "A Bit of Miniature Donkey History," www.Butterflatfarm.com/history.html.

22 Juliet Clutton-Brock, *Horse Power: A History of the Horse and the Donkey in Human Societies*, Cambridge, Massachusetts: Harvard University Press, 1992, p. 178.

23 *Ibid.*, p. 141. Taxonomists still debate equine evolution.
24 Richard Ellis, *No Turning Back: The Life And Death of Animal Species*, New York: Harper Perennial, 2004, p. 147.
25 *Ibid.*, p. 306.
26 "Feral horse (Equus caballus) and feral donkey (Equus asinus)," Australian Government, Department of the Environment and Heritage, 2004, at www. deh.gov.au. See also work by W. R. Dobbie, D. McK. Berman and M. I. Braysher, *Managing Vertebrate Pests: Feral Horses*, Canberra, Australia: Bureau of Resource Sciences, 1993. For information on the South African donkey crisis, see N. J. Jacobs, "The Great Bophuthatswana Donkey Massacre: Discourse on the Ass and Politics of Class and Grass," *American Historical Review* 108, 2001, pp. 485–507.

A Transcendent Reality Begins to Emerge

1 See "The Donkey Sanctuary": "Interesting Facts," at www. thedonkeysanctuary.org.uk/site/1/Interesting_Facts.html.
2 See La Maison du Baudet du Poitou at www.aventurier.fr/fr/france/poitou_charente/17_dec_baudet_dampierre/index.shtm
3 See Theodore H. Savory, "The Mule," *Scientific American*, December 1970, p. 6.
4 See Leah Patton, "American Mammoth Jackstock," The American Donkey and Mule Society, *The Saddle Mule News*, North American Saddle Mule Association, www.nasma.us/Jacks/.
5 See Jacques Roger *Buffon: A Life in Natural History*, Translated by Sarah Lucille Bonnefoi and Edited by L. Pearce Williams, Ithaca and London: Cornell University Press, 1997, p. 314. The 36 volumes derive from Buffon's four collective works of natural history from 1749 to 1788.
6 *Ibid.*, pp 330–332.
7 *Ibid.*, p. 320.
8 *Ibid.*, p. 240
9 *Ibid.*, p. 319.
10 Theodore H. Savory, "The Mule," *Scientific American*, December, 1970, p. 2.
11 Published in 12 volumes between 1668 and 1694. See, *Fables and Tales*, first published in English in London by A. Bettsworth, C. Hitch, and C. Davis in 1734.
12 Miguel de Cervantes Saavedra, *Adventures of Don Quixote De La Mancha*, Translated by Charles Jarvis, illustrated by Tony Johanot, London: S. O. Beeton, n.d., p. 130.

13 Miguel de Cervantes Saavedra, *The History of the most Renowned Don Quixote of Mancha: And his Trusty Squire Sancho Pancha*, Translated by John Phillips, London: Thomas Hodgkin, 1687, p. A7, last sentence paraphrased.

14 See //gallery.euroweb.hu/html/c/caravagg/02/13fligh 1.html; Caravaggio, *Rest on the Flight to Egypt*, 1596–1597, Galleria Doria-Pamphile, Rome.

15 S. M. McCandless, *The Burro Book*, Pueblo, Colorado: S. M. McCandless, Publisher, 1900, p. 4 of the Introduction.

16 H. H. Tammen, *Burros*, Denver, Colorado: The H. H. Tammen Curio Co., 1902, p. 2 of the Introduction.

17 Of course, Darwin was not referring to the art of painters, but of breeders. Charles Darwin, *What Darwin Saw in His Voyage Round the World in the Ship Beagle*, New York: Weathervane Books, 1978, p. 34. Baron Von Humboldt also described the sturdiness of the South American donkey breeds who seemed capable, he perceived during his travels in Venezuela, of living on nothing more than unrefined sugar, horses on maize. See John Smith, *Fruits And Farinacea: The Proper Food of Man*, New York: Samuel R. Wells, Publisher, 1872, p. 139.

18 See Terry N. Kinder, *Architecture of Silence: Cistercian Abbeys of France*, photographs by David Heald, New York: Harry Abrams, 2000.

19 See J. J. G. Alexander, *The Master of Mary of Burgundy: A Book of Hours*, Oxford: The Bodleian Library and New York: George Braziller, Inc., 1970. For depictions of equines, see: plate/prayer numbers 34, 65–66 and 75–76 for the distinctly noble portraiture of the donkey in the Lauds Visitation scene with St. Joseph, the Virgin, an ox and the ass, 80, 87–88 with the flight into Egypt illustrating the prayer at Vespers, the Virgin Mary and Christ child on the donkey surrounded by gold acanthus and other flowers upon gold, and 102–110, a unique depicture of a lady kneeling to milk the unicorn. See also, *The Hours of Mary of Burgundy: Codex Vindobonensis*, Vienna: Oesterreichische Nationalbibliothek, 1857, with English commentary by Eric Inglis, London: Harvey Miller Publishers, 1995. For material on the Jain panjorapors, see Michael Tobias, *Life Force: The World of Jainism*, Berkeley: Asian Humanities Press, 1992; and, Michael Tobias, "The Anthropology of Conscience," at http://www.psyeta.org/sa/sa4.1/tobias.html.

The Quiet Solace of Donkeys

1 See Stephen R. Kellert and Edward O. Wilson (eds.), *The Biophilia Hypothesis*, Washington, D. C.: Island Press, 1993. See also the March, 1990 Williams College Conference on "How to Bring about a New Cultural Commitment

to the Environment," and the discussion with E. O. Wilson, "Arousing Biophilia: A Conversation with E. O. Wilson," http://arts.envirolink.org/interviews_and_conversations/EOWilson.html.

2   See *Rubens & Brueghel: A Working Friendship*, by Anne T. Woollett, Ariane van Suchteden, with contributions by Tiarna Doherty, Mark Leonard and Jorgen Wadum, The J. Paul Getty Museum, Los Angeles, Royal Picture Gallery Mauritshuis, The Hague, in association with Waanders Publishers, Zwolle, The Netherlands, Los Angeles: Getty Publications, 2006, pp. 202–207, "Studies of Asses, Cats, and Monkeys," ca. 1615–16, Oil on panel, Vienna, Kunsthistorisches Museum, Gemaldegalerie, inv. 6985.

3   Tatiana Sikhotin-Tolstoy, *The Tolstoy Home: Diaries of Tatiana Sikhotin-Tolstoy*, translated by Alec Brown, New York: Columbia University Press, 1951, p 1.

4   Martin Kemp, *Leonardo*, Oxford: Oxford University Press, 2004, pp. 34–35. See also Giorgio Vasari, *Lives of the Most Eminent Painters, Sculptors & Architects*, Translated by Gasto, Duc De Vere, New York: MacMillan and Co. and London: The Medici Society, 1912.

5   Nº12362, Royal Windsor Collection, numbered 36 on the drawing. See Leonardo da Vinci, Instituto Geografico De Agostini, Novara, 1956.

6   "Die Geschichte vom weinenden Kamel," 2003, written and directed by Byambasuren Davaa, Luigi Falorni.

7   Jean-Claude Armen, *Gazelle Boy: A Child Brought Up by Gazelles in the Sahara Desert*, London: The Bodley Head, 1971.

8   Claudio Collodi, *Avventure di Pinocchio: Storia di un Burattino*, Illustrata da E. Mazzanti, Florence: Felice Paggi Publishers, 1883.

9   For this information, as well as discussion of the French Larzac plateau and its donkey shepherds, see "Some Information About The Donkey," at www.ane-et-rando.com/LAne/LAne2E.html.

10 Laurie Winn Carlson, *The Covenant of the Wild: Why Animals Chose Domestication*, New York: William Morrow, 1992, p. 15.

11 Laurie Winn Carlson, *Cattle: An Informal Social History*, Chicago: Ivan R. Dee Publishers, 2001, p. 28.

The Secret Imagination of Donkeys

1   See Louis-Rene Nougier, Martin Almagro Basch and Paolo Graziosi (Contributors), *Encyclopedia of World Art*, London: McGraw-Hill Book Company, 1966, Volume XI, pp. 587–614, plates 260, 262, 271, 272, 275 and 280. See also Andre Leroi-Gourhan, *Treasures of Prehistoric Art: Horse*, New York: Harry N. Abrams, Publishers, 1967, pp. 221–233.

2   From C. A. Wood (ed.), *An Introduction to the Literature of Vertebrate Zoology*, London, 1931, quoted in James Fisher, *A History of Birds*, London: Hutchinson's University Library, 1954, p. 14.

3   Fisher, *Ibid.*, p. 15.

4   *Ibid.*, p.15. Fisher magnificently concludes that such a mix of the real and the ideal is critical. Writing of Gilbert White's *The Natural History of Selborne* (1788), he says, "In White the nature investigator and nature-lover were inextricably confused; and many believe that the pursuit of truth in natural history will continue to be successful only so long as this benign confusion is preserved." (Fisher, p. 23).

5   F. A. Farrar, *Old Greek Nature Stories*, London: George G. Harrap & Company, 1914, p. 128.

6   Apuleius Apuleius, *Metamorphoses* or *The Golden Ass*, Thomas Taylor translation, London: Thomas Triphook and Thomas Rodd Publishers, 1822.

7   Other such works from the extensive children's library of curatorial donkey expert S. H. Price from www.oldchildrednsbooks.com, include: "Lloyd Alexander and Lester Abrams, *The Four Donkeys*, Austin: Holt, Rinehart and Winston, 1972; Angelo Valenti, *The Tale of a Donkey*, New York: The Viking Press, 1966; Paul Berna and Gareth Floyd, *The Mule on the Expressway*, New York: Pantheon Books, 1967; Bettina Ehrlich, *Cocolo's Home*, New York: Franklin Watts, 1950; Henri Bosco and John Ward, *Culotte the Donkey*, London: Oxford, 1978; Madeleine Brandeis, *The Little Mexican Donkey Boy*, New York: Grosset & Dunlap, 1929; Ann Nolan Clark and Agnes Tait, *Paco's Miracle*, Richmond: Cadmus, 1968; Ann Nolan Clark, illustrated by Leo Politi, *Looking-for-Something*, New York: The Viking Press, 1952; Vera Cleaver, *Sweetly Sings the Donkey*, New York: Lippincott, 1985; Lavinia Davis, Jean MacDonald Porter, *The Secret of Donkey Island*, Garden City: Doubleday Jr. Lit. Guild, 1952; Sophie Rostopchine, Comtesse De Segur, illustrated by Emma Brock, *The Wise Little Donkey*, Chicago: Junior Press Books, Albert Whiman, 1931; H. M. Denneborg, illustrated by Horst Lemke, *Grisella the Donkey*, Philadelphia: David McKay Company, 1957; Gerald Durrell, illustrated by Robin Jacques, *The Donkey Rustlers*, New York: The Viking Press, 1968; Joanna Galdone, illustrated by Paul Galdone, *Amber Day*, New York: McGraw-Hill, 1978; Paul Gallico, illustrated by Reisie Lonette, *The Small Miracle*, Garden City: Doubleday, 1952; M. Jean Craig, Barbara Cooney, *The Donkey Prince*, Garden City: Doubleday, 1977; Berta and Elmer Hader, *Midget and Bridget*, New York: The Macmillan Company, 1934; Marguerite Henry, illustrated by Wesley Dennis, *Brighty of the Grand Canyon*, Chicago: Rand McNally and Company, 1953; Madeleine

Hughes, illustrated by Rosalie Seidler, *Why Carlo Wore a Bonnet*, Boston: Lothrop, Lee & Shepard, 1967; May Justus, Robert Henneberger, *Jumping Johnny and Skedaddle*, New York: Harper and Row, 1958; Baroness Kos, K. Dombrowski. *Abdallah and the Donkey*, New York: The Macmillan Company, 1928; Robert Parker MacLeod, Dorothy Bayley Morse. *Tosco the Stubborn One*, New York: Thomas Y. Crowell Publishers, 1959; Anna Darby Merrill, Ella Dolbear Lee, *The Story of Mowie*, Chicago: The Whitman Publishing Company, Wig-Wag Series, 1920; Grace Moon, Carl Moon, *The Missing Katchina*, New York: Sundial Press, Young Moderns Bookshelf, 1939; Jean Morris, *The Donkey's Crusade*, London: The Bodley Head, 1983; Graham Oakley, *Henry's Quest*, New York: Atheneum, 1986; Leo Politi, *The Mission Bell*, New York: Charles Scribner's Sons, 1953; C. E. Pothast-Gimberg, illustrated by Elly van Beek, *Corso the Donkey*, New York: E. P. Dutton, 1963/1959; Diana Pullein-Thompson, Lili Cassel, *The Boy and the Donkey*, New York and London: Criterion Books, 1958; Janet Randall, Richard W. Lewis, *Burro Canyon*, Philadelphia: David McKay Company, 1964; Elaine Raphael and Don Bolognese, *Donkey and Carlo*, New York: Harper and Row, 1978; Anna Ratzesberger, illustrated by Kurt Wiese, *Donkey Beads*, Chicago: Albert Whitman and Company, 1938; Anne Rockwell, *The Girl with a Donkey Tail*, New York: E. P. Dutton, 1979; Helga Sandburg, illustrated by Morton Marian, *Bo and the Old Donkey*, New York: Dial Press, 1965; Alta Halverson Seymour, illustrated by W. T. Mars, *The Christmas Donkey*, Chicago: Follett Publishing Company, 1954; Charles Tazewell, illustrated by Franklin Whitman, *The Small One*, Philadelphia: John C. Winston Company, 1947; Anne H. White, illustrated by Don Freeman, *The Uninvited Donkey*, New York: Viking Press, 1957; Gerald Young, illustrated by W. Parkinson, *Chunk, Fusky, and Snout, A Story of Wild Pigs for Little People and Ups and Downs of a Donkey's Life*, New York: A. L. Burt, 1910.

8   Film review of *Au Hasard, Balthazar* by Bill Mousoulis, 2000. See http://www.senseofcinema.com/contents/cteq/007/balthazar.html.

9   See "Best Russian Documentaries" at www.tpotdf.ru/?id+films&lang+en&sect+2.

10   See *The Fables of Aesop, Paraphras'd in Verse: Adorn'd with Sculpture and illustrated with Annotations*, Second Edition, by John Ogilby, Esq., London: Thomas Roycroft Publishers, 1868. Fable XI -"Of the Boar and the Ass," pp. 29-30; Fable XXIV -"Of the Dog and the Ass," pp. 59-60, "...Then to his Master boldly he drew neer, At last charg"d him with a full Career: Then rising up, takes with a rough imbrace, About the Neck, offers to lick his Face..."; Fable XXXV -"Of the Horse and the Ass," pp. 82-84, "Daple so well

was known On his side all bout Bet, but"gainst him, none"; Fable XLVIII
-"Of the Horse and Laden Ass," pp. 117-118: In this Fable, the burdened ass
begs for assistance from a horse passing by who has nothing on his back. The
ass explains that the horse's sister bore to him a son, the mule, his hoped-for
heir, and points out that lacking any assistance, he, the ass, must lie down
and die. Full of pride, the horse ignores him. And the moral, "People that
under Tyrant Scepters live, Should each to other kind Assistance give..."; p.
118, Fable LXVIII -"Of Jupiter and the Ass," pp. 170-172; Fable LXIX -"Of
the same Ass," pp. 173-174; Fable LXX -"Of the same Ass and his Lion's
skin," pp. 175-177: This illustration by Hollar reveals the ass to be the same
as the most magnificent horse. And in his illustration to Fable XXIX -"Of
Birds and Beasts," p. 69, three equines side by side are laughing, expressing
intense curiosity, utterly at peace in the world.

11 *The Book of a Thousand Nights and a Night*, translated from the Arabic by
    Captain Sir R. F. Burton, edited by Leonard C. Smithers, illustrated by
    Albert Letchford, London: H.S. Nichols Ltd., 1897.

12 *Ibid.*, Volume 1, p. 33.

13 *Ibid.*, Volume 2, p. 340, footnote 1.

14 Two 16th century copper engravings after Hans Bol. Engraved by Gerard de
    Jode. Courtesy of the Fred R. Kline Gallery, Santa Fe, NM.

15 See Kenneth Clark, *Animals and Men: Their Relationship as Reflected in Western
    Art from Prehistory to the Present Day*, New York: William Morrow and
    Company, Inc., 1977, p. 69.

16 J. L. Borges, *The Book of Imaginary Beings*, Boston: David R. Godine
    Publishers, 1975, p. 35, the chapter entitled "The Ass with Three Legs."
    Borges also refers to a type of white donkey dancing across the moon.

17 See Jules Renard, *Natural Histories*, translated by Richard Howard,
    illustrated with lithographs and drawings by Toulouse Lautrec, Bonnard and
    Walter Stein, New York: Horizon Press, 1966, p. 107.

18 Reverend W. Bingley, *Animal Biography: Authentic Anecdotes of the Lives,
    Manners, and Economy of the Animal Creation*, London: Richard Phillips
    Publisher, 1805.

19 Robert Louis Stevenson, *Travels with A Donkey in the Cévennes*, Boston:
    Roberts Brothers, 1879, p. 235.

20 See *Kindness to Animals, or, the Sin of Cruelty Exposed and Rebuked*, revised
    by the Committee of Publication of the American Sunday School Union,
    Philadelphia, 1845. This book is part of a "kindness to animals" tradition
    in literature that includes such other works as the occasional series of 19th
    century children's books known as *A Mother's Lessons on Kindness to Animals*,

which included such moral tales as "The Ostend Donkeys," the "Old Coach Horse," "Sheep and Their Drovers," et cetera; Harriet C. Reynolds, *Humane Education: A Handbook on Kindness to Animals Their Habits and Usefulness*, Boston: American Humane Education Society, 1926; *Ladies" Gems, or, Poems on the Love of Flowers, Kindness to Animals, and the Domestic Affections. From the Most Approved Authors*, New York: E. Hutchinson Publishers, 1849; Emma E. Page, *Humane Education Ethical Culture Reader Book I. A Textbook for Teaching Kindness to Animals*, Arranged for Use in Public and Private Schools, Boston: Educational Publishing Co., 1909; and more recent works like Gerald Carson, *Men, Beasts, and Gods: A History of Cruelty and Kindness To Animals*, New York: Charles Scribner's Sons, 1972; and Lewis G. Regenstein, *Replenish the Earth: A History of Organized Religion's Treatment of Animals and Nature Including the Bible's Message of Conservation and Kindness to Animals*, New York: Crossroad Publishing Company, 1991.

21 John Urry, *The Works of Geoffrey Chaucer, Compared with the Former Editions, and Many Valuable MSS. Out of Which, Three Tales Are Added Which Were Never Before Printed*, London: Bernard Lintot, 1721.

22 Ulisse d'Aldrovandi, under the direction of Biancastella Antonino, *Les Animaux et les Creatures Monstrueuses*, translated from the Italian into French by Chantal Moiroud, Milan: Actes Sud/Motta, 2005, I. C. 159, p. 228.

23 David Perkins, *Romanticism and Animal Rights*, Cambridge: Cambridge University Press, 2003, pp. 108–115. See also Lean Sinanoglou Marcus, "Vaughan, Wordsworth, Coleridge and the *Encomium Asini*," *ELH (English Literary History)*, 42, pp. 224–41, Baltimore: Johns Hopkins University Press, 1975.

24 See Clifford S. Ackley, in collaboration with Ronni Baer, Thomas E. Rassieur and William W. Robinson, *Rembrandt's Journey: Painter, Draftsman, Etcher*, Boston: Museum of Fine Art Publications, 2003, pp. 72–73, 104–105 and 182–185.

25 Clare Lloyd, *The Travelling Naturalists*, London: Croom Helm, 1985, p. 77.

26 Mark Twain, *A Tramp Abroad*, London: Chatto & Windus, 1906, pp. 408–409.

27 Harold Jones, *The Visit to the Farm*, London: Faber and Faber, 1939, pp. 2-3; 6-7.

At the Edge of the Known World

1 See "The 'Hees' and 'Haws' of Donkey Brays," by David G. Browning and Peter M. Scheifele, 147th ASA {Acoustical Society of America} Meeting, New York, N.Y., May 25, 2004, www.acoustics.org/press/147th/Browning.htm.

2   Michael Tobias, *A Vision of Nature: Traces of the Original World*, Kent, Ohio: Kent State University Press, 1997.
3   R. B. Townshend, *The Tenderfoot in New Mexico*, London: John Lane, The Bodley Head, 1923. Chapter 17, "Spanish Mules," pp. 189–202.

The Donkey Paradox

1   AAEP *Care Guidelines for Equine Rescue and Retirement Facilities*, developed by the AAEP Equine Welfare Committee: M. Akin, DVM; J. Blea, DVM; D. Corey, DVM; M. Corradini, DVM; M. H. Gotchey, DVM; J. Jannsen, DVM; J. D. Kenney, DVM; T. R. Lenz, DVM; D. Markis, DVM; and N. Messer, IV, DVM, Lexington, KY: AAEP {American Association of Equine Practitioners}, 2004, p. 18.
2   *Ibid.*, p. 18.
3   This story of St. Francis and the donkey is one of many miracle tales recorded by the medieval Dominican Jacopo de Voragine in *The Golden Legend*.
4   See Kurt Barstow, *The Gualenghi –d"Este Hours: Art and Devotion in Renaissance Ferrara*, Los Angeles: The J. Paul Getty Museum, 2000, pp. 246–247 (JPGM, Ms. Ludwig IX 13, fol.193v.)
5   See "Sophismata" in the *Stanford Encyclopedia of Philosophy*: plato.stanford.edu/entries/sophismata. See also Jack Zupko, *John Buridan: Portrait of a Fourteenth-Century Arts Master*, Notre Dame, Indiana: University of Notre Dame Press, 2003.
6   See Michael J. Frank, Lauren C. Seeberger and Randall C. O"Reilly, "By Carrot or by Stick: Cognitive Reinforcement Learning in Parkinsonism," *Sciencexpress*: www.sciencexpress.org/4 November 2004/Page/1/10.1126/science.1102941.
7   See www.pseudopodium.org/ht-20010522.html.
8   See Simon Jacobson, "Balak: The Talking Donkey," at www.meaningfullife.com/oped/2004/07/01.04$BalakCOLON_The_Talking_Donkey.php. See also www.anunseenworld.com/balaamandthetalkingdonkey.html; and www.biblenews1.com/balaam/balaam.htm.
9   See www.bbc.co.uk/religion/ethics/animals/judaism1.shtml and www.foe.org.au/download/Judaism_and_Ecology_doc. See also www.jewishveg.com/schwartz.
10 See "Christ Story Bestiary," at ww2.netnitco.net/users/legend01/donkey.htm.
11 See Michael Tobias and Kate Solisti (eds.), *Kinship with Animals, Updated Edition*, Tulsa: Council Oak Books, 2006, p. 134. First published as *Ich spurte*

die Seele der Tiere, Stuttgart: Kosmos, 1997. See also Marc Bekoff's essay, "Animal Emotions and Animal Sentience and Why They Matter: Blending 'Science Sense' with Common Sense, Compassion and Heart," Chapter Three of J. Turner and J. D"Silva (eds.), *Animals, Trade and Ethics*, London: Earthscan Publications, 2006, pp. 27–40.

12 See Larry Rohter, "Currais Novos Journal: Pity the Donkey, a Beast That's Become a Burden," *The New York Times International*, May 26, 2001.

13 "The Donkey," (9 minutes) Vreme Film Studios, Environmental Video Center, 2002, www.abornat.org/501023.htm.

14 See www.stwing.upenn.edu/~durduran/hoca/hoca.htm.

The Genius of Donkeys

1 See Patricia D. Moehlman, "Status and Action Plan for the African Wild Ass (Equus africanus)" at www.iucn.org/themes/SSC/actionplans/equids/equidap.htm.

2 Jay F. Kirkpatrick and Patricia M. Fazio, "Wild Horses as Native North American Wildlife," www.wildhorsepreservation.com/resources/native/html. Presented as a Statement for the 109th Congress (1st Session) in support of H. R. 297, A Bill in the House of Representatives, House Committee on Resources, introduced January 25, 2005, "To restore the prohibition on the commercial sale and slaughter of wild free-roaming horses and burros."

3 See www.wikipedia.org/wiki/Horse; also see www.redlist.org/search/details.php?species=7961.

4 Dave Foreman, *Rewilding North America: A Vision for Conservation in the 21st Century*, New Mexico: The Rewilding Institute, 2006.

5 See Dr. Josh Donlan, "Re-wilding North America," published online in *Nature*, August 17, 2005. See news@nature.com.

6 RMR Ranch and Horse Dome, Wild Horse Foundation –Wild Horse and Burro Program (BLM) Facts; see www.wildhorseandburro.blm.gov/.

7 See Walter Brasch, "They're Shooting Horses (and Burros) Again, Aren't They?," *The American Reporter*, Vol. 11, No. 2,710, August 26, 2005. Mr. Brasch refers his readers to five excellent sources for obtaining more depth of information on the controversy. These are: The Humane Society of the United States (www.hsus.org/); the International Society for the Protection of Mustangs and Burros (www.ispmb.org/); the American Wild Horse Preservation Campaign (www.wildhorsepreservation.com/); the Alliance of Wild Horse Advocates (www.aowha.org/) and the Bureau of Land Management (www.blm.gov/).

8   *Ibid.*, Walter Brasch. See "California Deserts," Center for Biological Diversity, www.biologicaldiversity.org/swcbd/goldenstate/cda/actions. html. See also Scott Sonner, "Wild Horse Advocates Clash with BLM and Ranchers," AP, 6 July 2004, cited by Laurel Lundstrom, "No Home on the Range–Legal Menaces for Horses on Public Lands," Friends of Animals, Fall 2005, www.friendsofanimals.org/actionline/fall-2005/home-on-the-range. php.

9   "Get the Facts on Horse Slaughter," *The Humane Society of the United States*; www.hsus.org.

10 See Janet Ginsburg, "U.S. Wild Horses: Too Many Survivors on Too Little Land?," *National Geographic Today*, October 26, 2001. See also Christopher J. Stubbs, "Feral Burro Removal: New Solutions to an Old Problem," at www2.nature.nps.gov/YearinReview/yir98/chapter06/chapter06pg2.html. In addition, see www.desertusa.com/magjan98/jan_pap/du_wildburro.html.

11 See "A note on animal power and donkey utilization in Nigeria," by Mabayoje A. Ladeinde and Y. S. Ademiluyi in P. Starkey and D. Fielding (eds.), *Donkeys, People and Development: A Resource Book of the Animal Traction Network for Eastern and Southern Africa* (ATNESA), ACP-EU Technical Centre for Agricultural and Rural Cooperation (CTA), The Netherlands: Wageningen, n.d., 2004, pp. 220–221. www.atensa.org. See also S. O. Alaku, et.al., "Slaughter of donkey Equus asinus, 'The Ass' for meat: A survey of sources of meat in Equatorial Tropics of Southeastern Nigeria," *Tropical Journal Animal Science*, Vol. 5 (2) 2002, pp. 5–12. See also "FAO ramps up relief efforts in Sudan," see www.fao.org/newsroom/en/photo/; December 2, 2004, Rome: http://wire.agriscape.com/organizations/fao2004–12– 2.html, and, N. A., "Millions of Africans Near Starvation: UN," by *AFP, BBC, Reuters*, January 7th, 2006, www.universalrights, net/news/display. php?id=1681.

12 C. Z. Lei, et al, "Study on mitochondrial DNA D-loop polymorphism in Chinese donkeys," College of Animal Science and Technology, Northwest A & F University: *PubMed –PMID*: 16018258, May 2005, pp. 481–486.

13 See"Tibet Considering Culling Some Protected Animals," *People's Daily*, August 28, 2003, www.phayul.com/news/article.aspx?id=4830&t=1; See also "Tibet reports surprising population growth in rare species," *Expert*, July 15, 2003. www.chinaembassy.org.in/eng/ssygdzwt/ttxx/t60852.htm.

14 C. L. Lopez, et al, "Study of the genetic origin of the Mexican creole donkey (Equus asinus) by means of the analysis of the D-loop region of mitochondrial DNA," *Universidad Nacional Autonoma de Mexico, Tropical Animal Health and Production*, November; Vol.37, Supplement 1:173–88.

15 See "Herbivore Impact on Eurasian Landscape Ecology," in the website referred to by the topic-heading, "Functional Morphology, Ecology and Evolutionary Biology of Terrestrial Mammals," by PD Dr. Thomas M. Kaiser, Ernst-Moritz-Arndt University Greifswald Zoologisches Institut und Museum. http://www.evolution.uni-greifswald.de/eng/1.php.

16 See REBDIO/FAO: "FAO-CONFERENCIA ELECTRONICA No. 13," p. 8. www.redbio.org/newsredbio.asp?id=223.

17 Archaeological Solutions Ltd., See http://www.hertfordshire-archaeological-trust.co.uk/projects.html; also, see Ian L. Baxter, "A Donkey (Equus asinus L.) Partial Skeleton from a Mid-Late Anglo-Saxon Alluvial Layer at Deans Yard Westminster, London SW1," *Environmental Archaeology: The Journal of Human Palaeoecology*, Vol. 7, October, 2002, pp. 89–94.

18 See "Diversity Web," University of Michigan Museum of Zoology, "*Equus asinus.*" http://animaldiversity.ummz.umich.edu/site/accounts/information/Equus_asinus.html, pp. 5–6. See also: Juliet Clutton-Brock, *Horse Power: A History of the Horse and the Donkey in Human Societies,* Cambridge, Massachusetts: Harvard University Press, 1992, p.86, for a description and photograph from the Metropolitan Museum of Art of two hinnies in a scene from the XVIIIth Dynasty (1567–1320 BC) portrayal on the Tomb of Khaemhet, Thebes.

19 Juliet Clutton-Brock, *Ibid.,* p. 44, and p. 87, quoting from F. E. Zeuner, *A History of Domesticated Animals,* London: Hutchinson, 1963. For cuneiform translations, see p. 89.

20 Andrew Robinson, *The Man Who Deciphered Linear B: The Story of Michael Ventris,* New York: Thames & Hudson, 2002, p. 36.

21 See R. Paul Stevens, "A pilgrim's four days on the mountain of silence," at www.canadianchristianity.com.

22 See http://www.thedonkeysanctuary.org.uk/site/1/Donkey_Taxis.html

23 See below a list of some of some of the world's donkey sanctuaries:

Aruba – DONKEY SANCTUARY ARUBA, www.arubandonkey.org

Australia –THE DONKEY SHELTER INC., home.vicnet.net.au/~donkeysh
DONKEY WELFARE WITH HEART, ronda.thomas1@bigpond.com.au
GOOD SAMARITAN DONKEY SANCTUARY, donkeysanctuary@bigpond.com

Bonaire – BONAIRE DONKEY SANCTUARY, donkeyshelp@bonairelive.com

Canada – THE DONKEY SANCTUARY OF CANADA, www.donkeysanctuary.com
PRIMROSE DONKEY SANCTUARY, www.donkeyinfo.ca

Cyprus – FRIENDS OF THE CYPRUS DONKEY, www.donkeycyprus.com

India – ANIMAL RAHAT, www.animalrahat.com
DHARMA DONKEY SANCTUARY, www.dharmadonkeysanctuary.org

Israel – SAFE HAVEN FOR DONKEYS IN THE HOLY LAND, www.safehaven4donkeys.org

Italy – THE SARDINIAN DONKEY, www.sardiniandonkey.com

New Zealand – DONKEY WELFARE TRUST, TheNewZealandDonkeyWelfareTrust@xtra.co.nz

Spain – DONKEY SANCTUARY, www.burrosfelices.com
LOS BURROS FELICES, www.elrefugiodelburrito.com
NERJA DONKEY SANCTUARY, www.harrietsdonkeys.org

The Netherlands – STICHTING DE EZELSOCIETEIT, www.ezelsocieteit.nl

United Kingdom – THE DONKEY SANCTUARY, www.thedonkeysanctuary.org.uk
ISLAND FARM DONKEY SANCTUARY, www.donkeyrescue.co.uk
SCOTTISH BORDERS DONKEY SANCTUARY, www.donkeyheaven.org
THE TAMAR VALLEY DONKEY PARK, www.donkeypark.com

United Kingdom & France – N.E.D.D.I. DONKEY SANCTUARY, www.neddi.org

U.S.A. – BLACK BEAUTY RANCH, www.fund.org/ranch
HACIENDA DE LOS MILAGROS, www.haciendadelosmilagros.org
LONGHOPES DONKEY SHELTER, www.longhopes.org
PEACEFUL VALLEY DONKEY RESCUE, www.donkeyrescue.org
REDWINGS, www.redwings.org
TURTLE ROCK RESCUE, www.turtlerockrescue.org
WILD BURRO RESCUE, www.wildburrorescue.org

The National Miniature Donkey Association maintains a list of donkey sanctuaries and rescue organizations that is very helpful. See www.nmdasset.com/sanctuaries.php.

LIST OF ILLUSTRATIONS

75 *A Rustic Couple in a Landscape with Two Donkeys and a Dog*, ca. 1728, Italy. François Boucher, Courtesy Fred R. Kline Gallery, Santa Fe, NM

78, 79 "The Adventures of Sancho Panza." *As a Governor of Ebt, Island Godkoopenburg*, by Dr. T. C. Winkler, Amsterdam: Brothers Binger, 1872. Photo © 2006 Michael Tobias. All rights reserved.

81 *Historia Naturalis, De Quadrupedibus.* Johann Jonston. Amsterdam, 1650–53 Copper plate engraving. Photo © 2006 Michael Tobias. All rights reserved.

82 *Bonaparte Crossing the Alps*, 1848. Paul Delaroche. Oil on canvas. 289 x 222 cm. Louvre, Paris, France. Réunion des Musées Nationaux / Art Resource, NY.

85 *The Entry Into Jerusalem*, Benedictional, Unknown illuminator. Germany about 1030–1040 Tempera colors, goldleaf, and ink on parchment bound in white pigskin. 9⅛ x 6⁵⁄₁₆ in. © The J. Paul Getty Museum, Los Angeles.

86 *The Flight into Egypt*, detail from the Altarpiece of the Passion, Melchoir Broederlam © Musée des Beaux-Arts de Dijon.

87 *Adoration of the Shepherds.* Domenico Ghirlandaio, 1448-1494. Scala / Art Resource, NY. Location: S. Trinita, Florence, Italy.

88–89 *Rest on the Flight Into Egypt.* (1596-97). Caravaggio. (Michelangelo Merisi da). Alinari / Art Resource, NY. Location: Galleria Doria Pamphili, Rome, Italy.

90 *The Flight Into Egypt*, about 1480–1490.

Georges Trubert (French, active Provence, France 1469-1508). Tempera colors, gold leaf, gold and silver paint, and ink on parchment bound between pasteboard covered with red velvet. 14¼ x 3⅜ in. © The J. Paul Getty Museum, Los Angeles.

91 *Blue Donkey*, 1925. Marc Chagall. Artist Rights Society.

92 *Four Burros.* Thomas Sidney Cooper, 1803-1902. lithograph 1830s from book "Groups of cattle, drawn from nature," 1839. Private collection. Photo © 2006 Michael Tobias. All rights reserved

97 Osage woman at an Arkansas Ozark resort, ca. 1940. Osage Tribal Museum, Pawhuska, Oklahoma.

98 *Adobe Makers*, 1928. Jozef G. Bakos. Watercolor/graphite. Courtesy of the Collection of Cinco Pintores Association; Courtesy Gerald Peters Gallery, Santa Fe, New Mexico.

99 *White Man's Burden.* Charles M. Russell. Bronze. Courtesy Gerald Peters Gallery, Santa Fe, New Mexico.

100 *Mountain Farm*, 1928. Emile Armin. Courtesy Fred R. Kline Gallery, Santa Fe, NM.

101 From *Animated Nature, with Illustrative Scenery.* William Daniell. Published in London, 1809. Courtesy Ursus Books, New York. Photo © 2006 Michael Tobias. All rights reserved.

102–103 *St. Francis in the Desert*, ca. 1480. Giovanni Bellini. Tempera and oil on panel. 49 x 55⅞ inches. © The Frick Collection, New York.

108 *The Ass – Equus Asinus*, 19th century chromolithograph published under the direction of the Committee of General Literature and Education, Society for promoting Christian Knowledge. Photo © 2006 Michael Tobias. All rights reserved.

114–115 Rouffignac Cave, the Dordogne, France.

122–123 *Scene from a Midsummer Night's Dream. Titania and Bottom*, 1848-1861. Edwin Landseer (English, 1802-1873). Oil on canvas. 82 x 133 cm. Felton Bequest. National Gallery of Victoria, Melbourne, Australia.

126, 127 *The Fables Of Aesop, Paraphras'd in Verse*, by John Ogilby, Thomas Roycroft Printers, London, 1668. Photo © 2006 Michael Tobias. All rights reserved.

128–129, *Noah's Ark: Before the Deluge*. Hans Bol (Dutch, 1534-93), after. Engraved by Gerard de Jode (Flemish, 1509-91). Courtesy Fred R. Kline Gallery, Santa Fe, NM.

130–131 *Noah's Ark: After the Deluge*. Hans Bol (Dutch, 1534-93), after. Engraved by Gerard de Jode (Flemish, 1509-91). Courtesy Fred R. Kline Gallery, Santa Fe, NM.

134 *Travels with a Donkey in the Cévennes*, Robert Louis Stevenson, C. Kegan Paul, London, 1879.

136 *Asinus (Esel) Historiae naturalis de auibus libri 6*. Johann Jonston. Amsterdam (1650). Photo © 2006 Michael Tobias. All rights reserved.

138 *The Entry into Jerusalem*, about 1525-

1530. Simon Bening (Flemish, about 1483-1561) Medium: tempera colors, goldpaint, and gold leaf on parchment. 6⅝ x 4½ in. © The J. Paul Getty Museum, Los Angeles.

139 *The Terrestrial Paradise* (detail), 17th century. Private collection.

143 *A Tramp Abroad*. Mark Twain. London: Chatto & Windus, 1906. Photo © 2006 Michael Tobias. All rights reserved.

150, 186, 189, 190 Photo © The Donkey Sanctuary, Sidmouth, Devon, UK.

151 Photo © 2006 Carl Brune.

155 Ernie Franklin. Drawing. Ink and watercolor pencils. Courtesy of the artist, www.buffalomedicine.com.

168 *Saint Anthony of Padua*, Italy about 1469, Taddeo Crivelli, Italian,active about 1451-1479 Tempera colors, gold paint, gold leaf, and ink on parchment bound between wood boards covered with dark red morocco, 4¼ x 3⅛ inches © The J. Paul Getty Museum, Los Angeles.

172 *Nativity*. Melchoir Broederlam (1381-1409) Tempera on oakwood, 27 x 35 cm. Museum Mayer van den Bergh, Antwerp, Belgium. Eric Lessing / Art Resource, NY.

183 *Donkeys*. From *Animals After The First Masters For Examples In Drawing, Engraved Under the Superintendance of George Cooke, after Paulus Potter*, London, July 1, 1829, By Moon, Graves & Boys. Photo © 2006 Michael Tobias. All rights reserved.

188 © 2006 J.L.D Morrison IV.